How to Get Real About Dating

A Father and Daughter's Guide
to Finding Love at Any Age

Lauren and William Hamilton

Requests for such permissions should be addressed to:
Hamilton Writing
49105 Croquet Court
Indio, CA 92201

First paperback printing: September 2011

Ordering Information:
Quantity sales. Special discounts are available on quantity purchases by corporations, associations and others. For details, send all requests to the address above or email HamiltonWriting@gmail.com.

For more information about special appearances or to book events visit www.HowtoGetReal.com.

ISBN: 978-0-615-48642-0

Editor: Melissa Brandzel
Concept & Design: Celeste Byers & Faria Raji

Manufactured in the United States of America
10 9 8 7 6 5 4 3 2 1

Dedications

Lauren: I dedicate this book to my dad and step mom. Thank you for always being supportive, patient and open-minded.

To the thousands of strangers I spoke with as a server about life, love, and all that's in between—thank you for inspiring me with your amazing stories and words of encouragement.

William: Thank you to my wonderful kids and wife. You guys brighten my world.

Lauren and William: Lastly, this book is dedicated to all of the people who have been hurt by love. One day, you'll hit it off with an attractive stranger who will become your friend, and then your lover. And as you sip on some coffee one lazy afternoon, you'll realize that the hurt you've always felt deep down inside isn't there anymore.

Contents

Should I Go or Should I Stay?

The Convenience Package

It's Gettin' Serious

Me, Myself, and I

What If...

Epilogue

Acknowledgments

We are thankful to many people who showed us support in the past two years. This book is the result of friendships, advice, research, and resilience. Many individuals gave us words of encouragement, kicked us in the butt, or simply listened when we needed someone to lend us an ear. We'd like to thank all of them:

Jennifer Hamilton, for always being supportive and encouraging. Melissa Brandzel, for being a great editor. Heather Dubin and Matthew Mau from Undefeated Creative for their patience, talent, and precision. To those who gave their support: Sara Van Acker, Aaron Jackson, and Starvon Washington.

Preface

We know what you may be thinking:

Uh, I don't know you!

We understand. It totally comes with the territory when two people you don't know decide to give you advice about something as intimate as dating. It's natural to have questions or feel like no one knows what they're talking about except you.

We're not here to say we're right or you're wrong. The important thing is that you opened this book for a reason. Something brought you here, whether it's to get advice, have some fun, kick-start your love life, or you want something interesting to read on your lunch break. Whatever it is, you're with us, and we're glad to have you.

In life, sometimes we find ourselves inspired to do things because there's a feeling deep down in our soul that we *have* to do it. This could be skydiving, asking out a longtime crush, or eating chocolate-covered worms for the first time. You just couldn't see yourself going on without regrets unless you went for it. Well, that's how we felt about writing this book. In other words, we had to go for it.

The Inspiration behind This Book

Lauren: One day, I was sitting with my family at a restaurant in Venice Beach, California. My twenty-something brother, Aaron, kept looking over his shoulder at something in the distance. I was so focused on my lunch that I didn't bother to look. After a few minutes, he finally said to me, "Yo, Lauren, how about her?"

Reluctantly, I looked up and almost choked on my food in surprise. It's not that she was unattractive. In fact, she was very pretty. But there were some Caution Flags (explained in Chapter 3):

- ✓ *She was rockin' a stroller, and it had a baby in it.*
- ✓ *Two words: wedding ring.*
- ✓ *Not too nice to the waiter—detached, no eye contact, bossy.*

As a loving sister, I couldn't see my older brother with a woman like this—for obvious reasons. Yet, all he saw were nice legs and a banging body. I've definitely been there, but sometimes it's best to look in the other direction and run out the door.

Here's what I was thinking that day in the restaurant: *If Aaron thinks a married woman is good dating material, then he's probably always going to struggle to find a healthy love match.* It made me wonder: *Are we all doomed to pick the wrong partner or end up in a drama-filled, six-month affair like my brother and this woman had the potential to be in?*

I can't predict the future but what I believe is, as a young adult, **dating is hard**, especially when you have the Internet, texting, and other technological means of communication taking away from face-to-face interaction. It's hard to know the games and the rules. Actually—to be real—we young folks don't even own the game or know where to buy it. These are the things we're still figuring out as we become adults and make tons of mistakes. How are you supposed to know the best way to approach a cutie, or whether to ask someone out via Facebook, text, or a simple phone call? Sure, some of it is just learning through experience and creating your own path, but we all need an empathetic hand that can reach out and say, "Uh, that's probably not wise, bro" or "She's dope, go for it."

William: It's never good to smell your own piss.

Seeing my two sons and daughter date throughout the years has made me reflective. I have gained a lot of knowledge about relationships and love over the past few decades. With a few marriages under my belt, I can understand my children's arduous quest to find a Soul Mate and find themselves all at the same time. Honestly, it's a challenge that I don't miss.

Somewhere in my thirties, after two failed marriages and lots of dating as a Ladies' Man, I had to look at myself and figure out who I was, what was good and bad for me, and the importance of breaking the trend. Let's just say I had a lot of ballparks with way too many teams playing on the field. It was time for me to put my thoughts into action and learn how to focus on one lady at a time.

When you are a young professional, full of life, you think everyone sees you the same way. That's not true. You are simply falling into the familiar trap of thinking too much of yourself. In my mind, as a young man, everything had to happen fast and on my terms. I never wanted to be critical of myself. My grandfather would call this "smelling your own piss."

Somehow, it all came together and I became a mature and wiser man (I wish I could say it was a carefully mapped-out, forty-year plan, but you know better). Now, all this hard-earned knowledge gets dumped on my shorties when they need advice. Sometimes, what I express goes into use; sometimes, they completely ignore their Pops. But I know that my words reach their ears, even if it takes a while to sink in.

You may have a lot more "baggage" (kids, divorces, health issues) than you want to keep as the years go by and your age increases. However, there's no denying that getting older provides a ton of positives in the dating arena—one being that you have a better awareness of self-protection against toxic people and unhealthy boundaries.

My hope is that I can offer some words of wisdom as a "man of a certain age," mistakes 'n' all, and save you some time and heartache in the tough dating scene.

There's love out there to bring joy and blessings to your life. Don't let past mistakes and failures taint your attitude. If you've been single for years or feel like love is never going to happen for you, ditch those thoughts. Today is a new day. Focus on the present so that you can create a brighter dating future.

The Need to Have Conversations

William: Back in the day, people loved talking and opening up to each other. When I was on the market, there was nothing better than talking to a smart, attractive woman. Conversing and having face-to-face interactions established a natural communication style and allowed us to see if there was chemistry up front. These are things that can't happen on the Internet or through texting. Although I am out of the dating scene now, I still see that there are fewer conversations happening because I hear all about Lauren's stories.

Why is this problem happening? A lot of factors come into play, but that's not what is important. What matters is that we are growing more accustomed to not talking, and this is alarming. We have to get back to the basics and learn how to talk instead of how to avoid, be passive-aggressive, or say the opposite of what we mean. In my opinion, this is the only way to achieve ultimate relationship success.

How This Book Is Different

We're probably the most open-minded team you'll find. What you'll read isn't directed to one type of person or sex—it's for everyone who is looking for love. No one will be left out. Experienced or inexperienced with romantic relationships, you will feel right at home.

Unlike some other dating books, this one doesn't provide a "quick fix." If you don't get real with yourself and others, you'll get nothing out of this; there are no easy rides here. We aren't down with quickly scanning paragraphs and not thinking about these issues on a deeper level. We think you deserve better than that. It starts with you.

Don't Be So Hard on Yourself

It's easy to look in the mirror and be judgmental. You may find that you've made major dating mistakes or didn't handle a situation that well. That's okay. Both of us have done and said things that we aren't proud of, and that's all part of life. Though it may be hard to get over, the worst thing to do is keep thinking about those experiences and become your own bully. Everyone has room to grow, which makes us all ***beautifully imperfect***.

Let's learn from each other and take notice of the positives we all have. This will only allow dating to be more successful and enjoyable. So, forget about that one time you farted during a date and stunk up the whole restaurant. It happens.

Have an Open Mind

Just as we're coming into this with an open heart, we hope that you will too. The stories and experiences in this book represent people of all different backgrounds and walks of life. Ride with us and enjoy. Remember, close-mindedness isn't sexy.

Introduction

We're a father from the old school and a daughter from the new school.

In this book, we'll cover the *real* essentials of dating through advice, conversation, separate viewpoints, and thoughtful perspectives that go beyond the first steps of the courting process. It's not one versus the other or right versus wrong; rather, it is a discussion to show how times have changed and how they have stayed the same.

Dating isn't about playing games. It's about having a **game plan** that suits your needs and comfort level, no matter what your age. By starting out with a good strategy that fits your comfort level, your chances of coming away with a win increase dramatically.

What This Book Is and Isn't

*What it's **NOT***: A step-by-cheesy-step guide to help you get a date. You won't get any lame one-liners to use in a crowded bar or on a deserted island. If you need that type of coaching, pay some real cash and hire a personal coach.

We get into grown-up subject matters about dating, but sexual matters won't be one of them. If you need this type of help, go find yourself a professional sex therapist.

And lastly, no young kids allowed. For young teens looking for dating tips, ask your folks. They know what's up in that arena (hopefully).

*What it **IS***: We'll open your eyes about yourself and show you how to create a personalized game plan. This book is about checking the other person out, making the correct move(s), and knowing when to bounce or when to go the distance. Keeping your thoughts clear can be tough when your eyes are saying, "I gotta have it" or "This is way too hot to pass up." We're here to guide you through this journey and help you stay true to yourself.

We don't ask, but we TELL: The world is full of all kinds of people. What's normal? What's traditional? What's the majority? We can't speak in those terms. Why? The universe is too diverse and full of billions of individuals who are young, old, heterosexual, gay, brown, red, yellow, black, white, and so forth. Whew! This book reflects that. Paul McCartney and Michael Jackson got it right in their song "Black or White." Within these pages, you'll read about relationships from all kinds of backgrounds. You might be unique, but the rules of dating aren't—they're just **hard and tricky**.

Glossary

We'll refer to some terms and slang that we use or have heard on the scene. When you're out there mixing it up, everyone gets sized up and given a label. Young or old, there may be some of us who don't understand certain distinctions or have an awareness of what the labels mean.

Allow us to break it down.

William:

- A *Ladies' Man* attracts women naturally. These men radiate romanticism, style, intelligence, strength, a twinkle in the eye, and a gentlemanly nature. They may be hard to find, but when you do, it feels special to be around them all of the time. I was one back in the day and definitely knew how to make a woman feel like she was the only person in the entire world.

- *Playas* attract women, but they're usually out to get something. They will say what you want to hear and lie if it means getting out of trouble. Those attracted to *Playas* are playing with fire.

- *Good Guys/Good Gals* are safe. They typically have a good job, enjoy giving to others, and always play by the rules. These guys will not leave you high and dry. They're all about keeping their word and being there when you need them the most. The problem, usually, is that you never feel like you need them.

- *Niche Player* is someone you need for certain things like cuddling or an intimate love exchange (if you know what I mean). This person is generally good at one activity and should be assigned a label in your mind, like *Party Freak*, *Sportsaholic*, *Weekender*, or *Friends With Benefits*. With these types, you go nowhere fast, but it feels great in the moment.

- *Friend.* These folks attract the opposite sex, but it never starts with any romantic motives. It's always best to establish a friendship early, but there needs to be something in the back of your mind saying, "I could do this." The big trap is missing your cue and allowing it to turn into a brother or sister role. This is a bad label and waste of time for fellas or ladies trying to be successful on the dating scene.

Lauren:

- *Good Timers* are great peeps to go out with if you have nothing to do one night or you just need some good company who doesn't expect anything emotionally. You can always laugh and have fun with a Good Timer, but feel like a strong romantic connection isn't there or worth trying to create.

- *Not Serious* has no follow-through, but always pretends to want a serious romantic relationship with you. They may even seem like the total package and really pique your interest, but never back up what comes out of their mouth. These are common on the dating scene.

- *The One.* You get butterflies around this person. But it's also more than that. They have great morals, work hard, and match what you're looking for in life. Everything fits just right with this person and they make it known that you also fit just right.

- *Potential.* These are the guys and gals who often have amazing qualities, but they just aren't prepared at this time to be in a relationship or to date. This can be due to age, immaturity, or a lack of experience. Hopefully, they'll be ready and perfect for you down the road in life.

- *Play Thang.* You don't know where you go exactly with this person, but you go someplace amazing. Reality has left the building and you're okay with that for the brief period you two are together, which always includes a hot and steamy encounter.

Some of Our Golden Ideas

➢ Everyone gets labeled. Don't kid yourself.
➢ Know who you are. Be honest.
➢ Be willing to change and grow if you want more love and happiness.
➢ It takes one to know one.

Yeah, dating sounds a little like a sport. One in which the ball is always in your hands. Now, it's first and ten, you're out of the penalty box, you got a mulligan, and so forth. But like a sport, dating is never do or die. There is always another chance, another person, another experience. But with each experience, are you becoming better for it?

Let's Do This

Yup, life's tricky and hard, but that doesn't mean you can't master the game of dating. Now turn the page, dive deeply into this book, and get ready to start your dating engine.

1.
Out of the Cave

The caveman didn't go from drawing stick figures to masterpieces overnight.

It's no secret: The majority of singles are failing at the dating game and many have practically given up. When you get real about it, these failings relate to a large number of people simply going about it the wrong way, such as hanging out at whack places, having a poor appearance, or making bad choices. Eventually, what happens to these individuals is that they find refuge, a retreat into something safe and quiet, such as a home or even family. We call this a **CAVE**. Though it's probably tough to admit, most of us have a cave, such as a home or a job, but we can't let it trap us. Dating is already difficult on its own, and we can make even it harder by not finding a nice balance between *me* time and *the rest of the world* time.

Identifying your cave is the first step in getting real about what you need in your love life at this moment. There are some of you who genuinely feel like you have the time and energy to be on the scene. But as you read this chapter and do the exercises, you may realize that you have a major work cave and can't find time for someone special. Perhaps, you're always running away from anyone who makes you feel vulnerable. In this case, fear would be your cave. There are a variety of ways that we can create a cave in our lives.

That's why, just like a basketball game, you need a strategy—a plan for how you're going to find Cinderella or Prince Charming. This isn't a pickup game; it's the **Playoffs**. The competition is fierce and the ball is in your hands with a few seconds to go. Some of you will take the shot instead of passing it to an open teammate, while others will give up and not even try to shoot. Regardless, both outcomes leave you alone.

We want you to know when to put the ball down and when to pick it up. It's our mission to see you win the game of dating and believe in yourself, not to let that thought consume or intimidate you. Imagine how nice it will be when you're being interviewed after getting that win under your belt. Next to you will be your sexy date looking on with pride and admiration as you say: "I couldn't have done it without my teammates, or my Boo."

First, we'd like to share our stories with you.

William's Story

I learned how to stay out of the cave by observing what *not* to do.

Shortly after college, one of my friends—call him Rick—used to invite me over occasionally to hear the latest jazz releases on his state-of-the-art sound system. The music was outstanding. During the listening sessions, he would light up a "j" and feel like the music got even better. We would sit there for several hours admiring and analyzing each cut of the latest album he purchased. Somewhere during these sessions, we would have endless discussions about women, career goals, political and social issues, and exchange advice where we were having problems. Rick was cool, contemporary, and very intellectual. He was an account executive for a pharmaceutical company and seemed to be doing well. I considered him a good buddy.

> - W -
> "Philosophizing" is about as useful as an ape that knows sign language but can't really understand it.

But after several months of the same routine, I realized these sessions were all about *philosophizing* and nothing else.

Rick was living in a big-time cave. I realized he was all talk and no action. He was comfortable with his unfulfilled status in life. He had an *empty* relationship with his wife, never went out, didn't belong to any organizations, and wasn't taking his own advice on career advancement. Personal vices are personal. But in Rick's case, too much great music and good reefer were overly self-indulgent. They kept him prisoner in a cave. He definitely scored low in the game he was playing, landing nowhere near the Playoffs.

Let's break down another example. During the middle part of my corporate career, I was the director of marketing for a Fortune 500 company in San Francisco. Our department was led by a visionary and charismatic general manager named Hal. As department heads, we were young, energetic, and ambitious. Under Hal's leadership, his division always outperformed all others in the company by a wide margin. We were mavericks and could do no wrong. Most of us had the reputation of working hard and playing hard.

> **- W -**
> Never, ever pass up a good happy hour. You come out with a wallet that's not too much lighter, plus pockets that are heavy with numbers.

One of my managers, Bruce, took hard work to another level. He never had any play time. He was very thorough and analytical, and set very high goals for himself. I often told him to lighten up. "Hey Bruce, Hal and I are doing happy hour later with some peeps we met last week. These ladies are top-notch," I'd say. Bruce would agree to meet up, but never got there because he was finishing up a report or was on an extended call with someone in Europe.

Bruce was a tall, fit, Ivy League-looking dude. He had a quiet nature and warm smile. He could have been the Jesse James of the company. He was blessed with all the tools to be whatever he wanted—Ladies' Man, Playa, and the like. But instead, he was a Good Guy who didn't know how to find his social niche. He had lots of potential, but, by choice, was living in a *work* cave. (I really didn't mind Bruce's choice because it allowed me to get more than my fair share of the goodies from the happy hour forays.)

It was during the San Francisco years that I made a significant transition in style. I appreciated successful executives who had a certain presence. My grooming got cooler, my attire was more sophisticated, and the places I hung out were more upscale. Rick and Bruce were cool cats, but seeing them made me see what I didn't want: to hide. So, from that point on, dating was about getting myself to the next level and figuring out what I needed to do to make that happen.

Lauren's Story

I hid in food my entire life—really juicy and fatty foods at that. It's fair to say food was definitely my cave. Most thoughts that crossed my mind were "I wonder if there's anything good in the refrigerator" or "A few cheeseburgers would be nice right about now." Oh, and moderation? I had no idea what that word meant. Also, due to the

> - L -
> Being overweight might be worse than being a hoarder, but it wasn't to me. I would've loved a house full of cheesecakes and hot dogs.

fact that I often ate by myself, I became an expert at being alone, which only made my junk food addiction much worse. There was just no other option to fill that void of loneliness in my life. Plus, to be real, most fattening food tastes awesome.

Other kids would ask me to hang out all the time, but I would say no or that I was busy. Frankly, I had nothing to do but stuff my face full of chips and fries over episodes of *Oprah* at home. As I got older, my jean size hiked up, causing me to stay at home even more since I was so uncomfortable with my body. Over time, I spent less time going out and hanging with the few friends I had. When I reached high school, I started to feel like food was my only homey, when, in fact, *I had made the choice to isolate myself.* All of those burgers and chips didn't force their way into my mouth—I put them there.

It wasn't until college that I decided something had to change. I was finally able to realize that *I had the power to improve my life.* I couldn't continue to live on the inside, stuck in my own fear and reclusive lifestyle. Later in this chapter, I will tell you how my social and dating life changed after this eye-opening moment.

The Cave Survey

You're a Cave Person if . . .

➢Your "going out" clothes are the same as your work clothes.

➢Work is fun, and fun is *hard* work.

➢On your days off, you just sleep (alone), do laundry, and surf the Internet.

➢You enjoy cooking nice meals and then eating them alone.

➢Your legs are hairier than Chewbacca's.

➢The name you say the most is a character from your favorite video game.

➢#2 on your to-do list is to watch the entire collection of *The Lord of the Rings* films . . . tonight.

➢You like to talk to yourself, and just yourself.

➢Your idea of a good night out is chatting with the creepy guy at the Laundromat over Coke and dirty drawers.

➢If offered a million dollars to explain what the weather's like outside, you'd have no clue.

➢You spend more than two hours a day on the couch watching television.

➢Your dog now gives you an "Oh, you again" look every time you walk through the door.

➢There's a rumor spreading that you're a recluse—started by the eighty-two-year-old woman next door.

➢When a friend asks if you'd like to see a movie, you respond, "What time are you coming over?"

➢You'd rather go home and watch *Animal Planet* than join friends for dinner.

➢The only time you use your cell phone is to order takeout or to see when that Amazon purchase is arriving.

Yeah, we're totally making fun of Cave People. But if you're thinking, "It's kind of true," then don't stop here. We're going to go deeper and see where you're really hiding.

Where You Stand

Let's focus on what areas need some attention. Answer these questions and add the totals for each section. At the end, we will tell you where you rate as a Cave Person.

On the statements below, write one of the following numbers that best describes you:
1 – Never
2 – Rarely
3 – Sometimes
4 – For the most part
5 – Always

Part A
- ➤ ___ I prefer solo assignments to working on a team.
- ➤ ___ I take most things seriously and don't usually laugh at myself.
- ➤ ___ I spend an hour or more per day surfing the Internet.
- ➤ ___ I usually stay quiet at work and make no effort to know my co-workers.
- ➤ ___ Company parties are awful; I'm afraid to let go and enjoy myself.
- ➤ ___ The thought of getting dressed up and having fun with friends doesn't really appeal to me.

Part B
- ➤ ___ I prefer noise and bright lights vs. the quietness and routine of a less active lifestyle.
- ➤ ___ I usually eat meals at a restaurant, friend's house, or another location other than my crib.
- ➤ ___ I rarely spend more than ten minutes a day on the Internet.
- ➤ ___ My crib is simply a place to crash, change clothes, and grab a bite.
- ➤ ___ My place is usually equipped for entertaining (i.e., wine, candles, music).
- ➤ ___ I usually bring dates over and try to seal the deal.

Part C

➤ ___ I feel lonely most days, and like to deal with my emotions alone as opposed to calling friends to feel better.

➤ ___ When friends invite me out to an event, I make an excuse not to go.

➤ ___ I frequently eat meals at home.

➤ ___ I tend to call myself a homebody.

➤ ___ I have at least two hangouts where they know me.

➤ ___ When I'm out, I stand by myself or solely focus on my friends.

Part D.

➤ ___ Good health. Trim and fit, sparkling smile, and *nice* breath!

➤ ___ Style. Clothes, nice ride, body language, good conversation.

➤ ___ Attitude. Total confidence to go anywhere and hit on anyone.

➤ ___ Finances. Money is not funny.

➤ ___ Friends. Always attend important events, buy them b-day gifts, and reach out on a regular basis just to check in.

If your score is **above 30 on Parts A & C**, you have Cave Person issues and trouble interacting with people in general. If you're being real with yourself, you have anxiety being in group situations, socializing, and just hanging out with friends and associates. Your call to action? Well, if it's a particular group you don't like, find one that you do like. If you aren't diggin' the project or work environment, seek a change immediately. In other words, address the source of your anxiety, fix it, and start putting

> - L -
> If you own more than 30 video games and manage to play them all each week, it may be time to go to Video Game Rehab.

yourself out there. Ultimately, your challenge is learning to say yes when social opportunities arise.

Lauren: Saying yes is easier said than done. I can relate as a writer and someone who loves to be at home. But we have to put ourselves out there with a positive attitude. For example, my colleagues invited me out to karaoke recently, and I totally wanted to chill at home. Instead, I said, "Sure, I'm down." And it turned out to be a great time. I met some cool people I didn't know well at work, got closer to others, and enjoyed the terrible singing. By the end of the night, I was glad I went out as opposed to hiding out at home in my pajamas.

If your score is **below 30 on Parts B & D**, you've got Cave Person issues that reside within yourself. You like going out and being in social situations, but it's too much work. So, guess what? You find pleasure and hide in your own personal stuff like video games or watching movies. It may be your attitude, money, or health that keeps you in that cave. Based on your answers, it's probably easy to see where you came up short in a few areas. Ultimately, you need to push back from the creature comforts of cave living.

- W -

If you aren't a Cave Person, it's still good to know about them. You may be interested in someone like this, and knowing how to bring them out of their shell could be useful.

Feeling odd about your score? Good. We're starting a new kind of conversation here, and sometimes you may feel a bit uncomfortable. This survey is meant to inspire a positive outcome—to see you rock out the dating world. In order to get to that destination, a few things have to happen:

1. Commit yourself.
2. Set some personal goals.
3. Work every day to achieve these goals, one step at a time.

I'll Have the . . .

After doing the survey, some of you may be thinking, "Of course I'm a Cave Person, I work all the time!" or "I'll never go to a club because I hate them!" We're not saying you have to change who you are or that you have to force yourself to do things that sway from your authentic self. That's never a good thing and will definitely not attract a good match for you. However, you can still be yourself while changing up your routine to be more visible and active in order to find love down the road.

Think of the times you've gone out to a restaurant with friends, family, or colleagues. Everyone has different tastes, drink preferences, allergies, and other special demands that have to be met by the food options. For example, I (Lauren) have a friend who is a vegan, and I always make sure to research places that accommodate her diet whenever we go out together. Every time I mention this to peeps, they always comment about how hard it must be to track down the right places. But, ya know what? I never fail to find a place. Do I want to eat vegan food? Not usually, but there hasn't been one occasion in which I didn't enjoy my meal.

> **- L -**
> If something is new or different for you, try it at least once. Chances are, the experience will be a nice one.

In life, you'll always come across options to fit your unique wants and desires. Though every item on the menu won't appeal to you, there are a number of them that will. You may not like going to a happy hour with friends, but perhaps the idea of going on a hiking extravaganza excites you. No matter what you're craving, there are ways to fulfill your needs. One way to do this is by focusing in on the things you like to do and then creating your own strategy for getting back into the sunlight.

Getting Back Into the Sunlight: Visibility Menu

Everyone has different preferences in life. What turns you on may make someone else nauseous. That's why it's important to come up with places, events, and hobbies that you're comfortable with to get you out of your cave.

How do you figure this out? One option is by creating your own personalized *Visibility Menu*.

It's hard to get hit on if you're at home watching soap operas all day or spending eighty-five percent of your time at work.

Lauren: As a young person, my apartment isn't the only thing that runs the risk of being a cave. It can be texting, being on my laptop for hours, or even chatting and surfing sites like Facebook and MySpace. As a whole, most peeps have become less focused on face-to-face interactions since technology has improved so much in recent years. That's why I think the Visibility Menu, especially for the younger crowd, should focus more on talking, approaching, and interacting with others *in person.*

> **- L -**
> Don't let your finances tie you down. Budget your outings to maximize your time out. Never overspend your quota, because there's nothing worse than your money getting funny.

- Go to a bookstore, grab a cup of coffee, sit down, and make a genuine effort to start a conversation with someone you don't know.
- Call a friend and ask him or her to go have lunch that week.
- Go to a club and dance the night away with random people. Oh, and don't leave without at least one number.
- If you don't have a job, network your tail off 24/7 to get one. Being at work makes you get to know new faces.
- Smile at everyone you pass.
- Join an activity or a sports team to be active and meet new individuals.
- Start using Skype instead of an instant messenger so you can see who you're talking to.
- Eat at a new restaurant once a week, whether alone or with someone else. Try to have others join you most of the time.
- Buy a nice, well-fitted item of clothing once a month and take a friend. You'll have more confidence and look even better after doing this.

- ➤ Join a gym and go three times a week. You may hate it, but you'll have more energy and feel better after a great workout.
- ➤ Invite peeps over for a glass of wine, game night, or a movie twice a month.
- ➤ Go out with friends when they invite you somewhere at least eighty-five percent of the time.
- ➤ Purchase a popular perfume/cologne and use it daily, even when you're running quick errands. You'll turn a few heads for sure.

Don't force yourself to chill at a café if you prefer joining a wine tasting group.

William: When you've been in and out of the dating scene as a mature person, time is at a premium, and you don't like wasting it. You must get up and leave your cave immediately. *Your clock is ticking.* Every minute lost watching cable news and reruns on television must be seriously curbed. Even if you don't have a major isolation problem, it's still good to know how to stay in the game.

> **- W -**
> Lauren and I agree that like attracts like. If you're positive and open-minded, chances are you'll meet others like that.

- ➤ Check your appearance. Spiff up the easy stuff. Try a new hair salon (guys, too), update your attire (separate business and social), keep the weight off, and no smoking. If I can quit, so can you.
- ➤ Find several restaurants and hit them at least once a week. You need to stay at least two to three hours (avoid quickie ins/outs), and make yourself talk to people on every visit.
- ➤ Hang out with younger people. You need to be young at heart. Older people often fall into the trap of gradually closing down their activities, becoming critical of things they don't understand, and sweating the small stuff. ***You attract what you radiate.***
- ➤ Select friends who make you laugh, be more active, and think. Generally, most people won't match up on

all these levels. That's okay, just recruit and socialize with them accordingly. I have golf buddies, party pals, and simply interesting friends. We discuss all kinds of topics. Brain activity keeps you energized.

➤ Use *upscale* matchmaking/dating services. Mature people often have many demands on their schedule, such as work, appointments, and family. Freelancing in public places alone requires a lot of time, and the disappointments are high. Many matchmaking companies can save you a lot of time and give you volume and quality on your schedule.

Now that you have a handful of options and examples, come up with your own Visibility Menu of at least three to five items.

Create a Visibility Menu that caters to your interests and comfort level.

My Visibility Menu
1) _____
2) _____
3) _____
4) _____
5) _____

Before and After

Here's an idea of how your normal routine should change after utilizing your Visibility Menu.

Before

You get off work, feel tired, and choose to sit in front of the television until you pass out after eating a frozen dinner.

After
You get off work and chill at home for an hour. After that, you hop in the shower and meet a friend for dinner at a nearby restaurant.

Before
A work project has you in the office for more than eighty hours a week. "At least I have a job" is what you tell yourself to keep from going over the edge.

After
Your co-workers invite you for drinks at a new hot bar with a banging happy hour. You take them up on their offer and hang for an hour.

Before
Every time you have a day off, you drive two hours away to spend it with your family.

After
You sign up for a weekly interactive class, such as cooking or studying a new language.

Before
Every morning you go for a nice jog alone.

After
Two nights a week you hit up a popular neighborhood gym for a run on the treadmill.

Before
You play video games two to four hours a day by yourself.

After
There's a huge video game convention coming to town and you decide to go so that you can socialize with other gamers.

What to Do Next

Sometimes things are easier said than done. You may still have some hesitation and fears, even as you sit in your chair with a completed survey and a personalized Visibility Menu all ready to go. Perhaps you just ***aren't ready to order***. Don't worry—fear isn't a bad thang. It's normal when you try something new.

Here's how we took things to the next level and got out of our caves.

Setting Goals: Lauren

At the age of nineteen, when I was a lonely freshman in college, it finally hit me that I needed to change the path I was on.

One day I was in bed alone with a bag of potato chips, watching a Lifetime television movie. During a commercial break, I saw an advertisement for an aerobic workout video. The program looked kind of cool, but I didn't pay any real attention to it. Exercise wasn't my thang. But when I saw the same ad the next day, I said, "Aight, if I see this thing three more times tomorrow, I'll buy it." Sure enough, I did (which wasn't shocking since I watched at least four hours of television a day). After I received those DVDs, something clicked inside of me. I was ready to make the change, and I did just that. I exercised to those workout videos almost every day for more than six months. I also changed my diet and started eating healthier foods.

That was the beginning of my physical transformation, which brought about an emotional change, too. In the next year, I lost more than eighty pounds, bought new clothes, and learned how to put makeup on for the first time. When people asked me to hang out, I said yes because I felt good about myself. I started to have fun, enjoy life, and date. Of course, putting myself out there felt strange at first, but that didn't last long. I was too focused on looking and feeling great in my new skin. I went from a size "let's not talk about that" to a size "oh, snap." No one could stop me from smiling, getting to know people, and doing things that made me feel great while also making time for school and family.

Once I felt comfortable with myself, I started going out. I made a list of simple things I always wanted to do—hang out with new roommates, go check out a bonfire at the beach, meet new folks, hike, and so forth. At first, it was tough. I didn't find it natural or easy to talk to people a lot. Five words and I wanted to scoot on back home to my Lifetime movie. I simply found it tiring. But as time went on, I grew to come close to people and made good friends. Many of them I talk to on a regular basis, including my current roommate, Glenn. Now I run my mouth and always pour my heart and soul out to close friends. I made commitments to myself and kept them until they became second nature.

> **- L -**
> We all have the potential to find the *Oh, snap* that's inside each and every one of us.

For those of you who are sitting on your couch wishing the pounds off, or hoping that you'll suddenly feel great on the inside and outside without putting in any effort, things probably won't change. You and only you can change yourself. Whether you're suffering from depression, a breakup, or a physical issue, try your best to take charge of life and be the best you can be.

Let's Break It Down
We are all GOLD

Lauren: My journey has made me see how much we all deserve to be valued and cherished for who we are as individuals. No matter your weight, shoe size, race, whatever—you are worthy of the best since that's exactly what you are. There may be people in your life telling you otherwise, but they're just *haterz*. If you keep in mind how dope you are, you'll begin to see the gold not just in others, but also in yourself.

Setting Goals: William

After my first marriage ended, I found myself back on the singles scene and a full-fledged Ladies' Man. Professionally, I maintained my commitment to becoming a successful corporate executive. But I was constantly seeking companionship with quality women. It was during these times that I started reading a lot of self-help books, meditating, observing successful people, critiquing myself, and making adjustments.

> - W -
> You have to look good in order to feel good.

What did making adjustments mean to me? First, it was important to be comfortable with my appearance—good dental and skin hygiene, hairstyle statement, and attire that always made me *one up*. Fate led me to a clothing store where I met a distinguished European salesperson in the men's suit department. He had a passion for quality clothing and insisted on putting me in good stuff. He would make up sales discounts and do layaways to accommodate my budget limitations. He opened my eyes to designer suits, silk ties, wool, cashmere, linen, formalwear, and the like. We became good friends and my wardrobe went to a higher level. I made a point of working out and jogging to stay in shape. Plus, I always felt better as a result.

But once you get past a person's appearance, there has to be a conversation. Being knowledgeable about current events and having views about the world are great. However, you have to be a conversationalist. It's important to be able to size up the other person and quickly determine how to engage them in enjoyable small talk. (That's one of the things a Ladies' Man does very well.)

So, setting goals means *doing something to improve yourself.* I tell everyone on the way up to avoid the trap of coasting through life in predictability and mediocrity because these things usually leave us feeling sad and unfulfilled. Take risks, set goals, and also go beyond that and put them into action. With this mindset, you'll eventually find your ideal dating match.

Chapter Summary

William: The clock is ticking. Life isn't a dress rehearsal. Let's get going. Stop eating alone so much, watching old episodes of *The View* on your DVR, and listening to your family boss you around. You have to do what's best for you, even if it's against your mother or father's expectations.

Lauren: Don't confine yourself within four walls. Tomorrow is a new day. It's never too late. When I think about getting old and grey, I ask myself, *Where would I want to be?* The answer never involves a television, Facebook, my iPhone, or my computer. I always think the same thing, which is *with someone I love by my side.*

William's Old School Wisdom	Lauren's New School Wisdom
Tweak your look. Hair and teeth. Stay fit and make sure your clothes represent quality and style.	Make sure the peeps in your life are bringing you up, not down.
Be young at heart. Age is just a number. Active, contemporary, positive people are more enjoyable to be with.	Treat yourself to something nice once a week, like dinner or a manicure. It's fun and gets you used to being treated well.
Find your passion and do something! Join an organization that energizes you. Focus on a subcommittee and get deep into it.	Join a social networking website such as Facebook or MySpace for friends and maybe dating candidates. Just don't get addicted. Less than thirty minutes a day!
Find an activity—i.e., golf, traveling, community work—that gets you out interacting with people.	Talk to random strangers to get out of your comfort zone.
Practice saying "yes" when someone asks you to do something. Take a few risks.	Mom and Dad don't count as "going out" buddies.

Consider other options for making social contacts, such as using quality Internet matchmaking services. Be careful, but this could save you time.	Once a month, do something crazy (as long as it's legal).
Roll solo when you're on the hunt. Hanging with the guys and talking sports is a big blocker with ladies.	Consider talking to a counselor about how to cope with anxiety if you have it when hanging out at places or while talking to new people.
Don't be afraid to approach a good-looking lady. They like bold, confident guys.	Get passionate about a group, organization, or public figure that you identify with on some level.

What Every Older Person Needs to Know
for those on the prowl

➢ Get a Facebook account and use it not only to flirt, but also to be entertained. It may feel weird and pointless at first, but give it time. There have been plenty of couples who have met via this website.

➢ If you don't know how to text, learn. Then, send at least five texts a week to someone you know to get into the routine. Once you start dating, you'll look hip and trendy typing away on your phone. Plus, it's an easy and quick way to send a few sweet words.

➢ Not having time for breakfast one morning is normal, but not getting **down and dirty** for three or four years isn't. Don't forget to give yourself some loving and go on a few dates, even if you're working an insane job.

➢ If you're interested in someone younger, make sure to not be belittling or judgmental. That's not hot or very nice.

➢ Do something completely out of your comfort zone once a week, like salsa dancing, going to a happy hour, or participating in a fundraiser.

➢ There's no need to wait a million years to have the kids meet your new Boo for a few hours. The kids will appreciate the introduction in the end.

➢ Go personal ad crazy by using Match.com, eHarmony, Yahoo personals, and other dating websites. You can never have too many, but make sure to check them biweekly just in case someone is interested and trying to contact you.

➢ Joining a gym is sexy. Especially if you go at least three times a week. Actually, make it four.

◆◆◆
2.
What's Your Top 5?
◆◆◆

You may be the only one with an umbrella, but at least you won't get wet.

It's important to know what you're looking for in a potential partner as you explore the dating scene. Another important factor is being able to stay focused when you have someone sexy and cute staring at you, which is why we recommend having a list of criteria always etched in your brain, something we call your **Top 5 List**.

You may feel it's not important to think about this now, but by not thinking about it, you risk getting involved with the wrong type of person who can lead you way off course in the romantic arena. For example, if you don't want to invite a gold digger into your life, then knowing that you want a financially independent person is important to bring into your awareness.

Think back on all the times you went to a local coffee shop in the morning. On your way there, you probably thought about what you wanted. "I'm craving an espresso and a slice of lemon cake." "That raspberry Danish pastry has my name all over it." Before entering the building, you knew what you wanted and didn't sway on that decision once you walked in the door, even after seeing the other delicious options. It's not a surprise that most of us have an easier time deciding what we want for breakfast than what we look for in a love match. Most of us give way more thought to the former than the latter.

We're going to share our own Top 5 List with you. One comes from a young person's point of view (Lauren) while the other comes from an older one (William). We'll explore how the things you want in your twenties definitely change in your late thirties and beyond. Then, we'll wrap things up by having you create your own list to store in the back of your mind as you begin exploring the dating scene.

The List

Lauren's #1: Spontaneous

> - L -
> Stuck on what to do for fun? Hit up a casino or comedy show. Get a massage or take a day trip to an amusement park or a museum.

Dating should be fun. Well, at least ninety percent fun and ten percent serious in the beginning. There should be no guilt trips, intense planning discussions, passive-aggressiveness, stress, or concerns (unless it involves how to do something sweet or romantic). As a young woman, I like to be treated well and know that the person I'm dating can take a joke, laugh easily, and not sweat the small things. Due to the fact that I'm so busy with work and finding time to make sure that I fulfill my responsibilities, any extra time goes to lighthearted activities. When I am able to go out and kick it, I want to do new and different things that put me outside of my comfort zone or simply relax my overworked body.

A few years ago, when I was in college, I was going out with a woman for several months, and every week I would offer ideas for new things we could do. One time I suggested that we have a wine night, even though I knew she stayed away from it since, as an opera singer, it wasn't good for her throat. I'm thinking to myself, *Okay, that means she only drinks on special occasions.* So, one night I brought over champagne, crackers, and ice cream as a surprise. I was beyond excited as I got onto the subway to go to her apartment in Harlem. I just knew she was going to run into my arms when she saw my surprise. Who doesn't want to drink champagne with their sexy date? When I showed her the surprise, her response was "You know I can't drink that." I tried to get her to drink a little bit and at least try the ice cream I bought, but I didn't get a positive response from that either. The rest of the night was spent watching a boring movie as the champagne sat in the refrigerator. I can think of many words to describe that night, and "fun" isn't one of them.

But that was a good experience for me because it made me pinpoint what I needed at that stage in my life: fun and adventure. Spontaneity can be a good quality to look for in a lover, whatever your age. Don't you want someone who's willing to relax and drink a little champagne, or let loose and drink a few beers? Really take a moment and think about that, because I never did and it bit me in the *you-know-what*. And, hey, when you're working more than forty hours a week in a high-stress environment, going out with someone you can grab a drink with on a moment's notice is the best thing in the world.

> **- L -**
> It's never a good sign when the person you're dating doesn't give you a kiss when you see each other. You're better off snuggling with your pillow in bed alone than dealing with that.

Plain and simple, things shouldn't be complicated and stressful in your dating life, especially as a young adult. Dating should be relaxing, kind of like your favorite hotel. It's something that allows you to let your hair down, relax your body, and be yourself. If it ain't doing that for you, it might be time to check out of that relationship.

William's #1: The "It Factor"

> **- W -**
> Patience is good, but not boredom. If a person just doesn't do it for you, it's better not to force it.

What does this mean? It's all about being *multifaceted*. I must be honest: Guys look at most women the first time in terms of whether they want to have sex with them or not. This isn't something I just made up—it's true. Even Donald Trump has been known to make this point. At my age, I prefer attractive, girl-next-door, stylish-looking ladies. A beautiful face does not impress me. I shy away from over-the-top dressers: extremely short, too tight, or overly revealing clothes; big hair; and excessive makeup. These are big turnoffs. If a lady has "it," there is no need to overly advertise. It's all about the *look*!

Whether it's a One Nighter, Weekender, or Long Termer, there has to be a "hot factor." Does this person light your fire? Or make your blood boil? If you are a Ladies' Man or Playa, you can assess your date accurately after a drink or two and a few minutes of small talk. Good Guys and Good Gals need lots of time and usually seek follow-up dates to figure things out, but give them a shot. Sometimes it takes time to find that spark, or it can come unexpectedly.

Two important underlying ingredients in terms of the "It Factor" are *mutual attraction* and *reciprocity.* Have you hit on someone who turned your head, only to find out that the person is preoccupied or not feeling the same vibes? But he or she looks so good that you try to force the action? You're giving one hundred percent and the person is giving you nuthin'. Some indicators of this are: (1) you do most of the talking, (2) you call and pursue, but get limited replies, and (3) everything has to be on their terms and all about them. If the other person is attracted to you, there will be responsiveness and reaching out. You can tell. Don't fool yourself. Be real.

Lauren's #2: Not Interested in an *Immediate* Major Commitment

Say no to the "D"

There's nothing worse than a lot of pressure, particularly if you lead a busy life. We all have enough of it in our lives. Beyond paying my monthly bills, career, friendships, and eating, I don't live by any sort of **deadlines**. I just don't have the energy or desire to add another component to my plate besides the occasional family gathering and going out from time to time. So, someone who starts to bring up marriage, kids, or anything along those *serious* lines is scary since we're just starting to get to know each other.

The person you're seeing should fit along mellow and cool lines. Now, I'm not talking about dating a Filler type. No, no, and no. I'm talking about an individual who understands that you have a lot of responsibilities and goals in life, and that you are looking for a flexible partner who will respect this lifestyle and not ask for a huge commitment with a time requirement.

Imagine getting a job offer as a manager and having to balance that with a marriage and kids. For some, it's appealing, and that's completely fine. But if you know you're career-driven and don't want a family right away, you have to honor that or you won't be happy.

Marriage and other long-term commitments are no joke and should be taken seriously. If you're dating someone who is showing signs of wanting to settle down soon, and you know deep down in your heart that you aren't ready for that, take a step back for a second. The same applies to peeps who have a crush on a guy or a gal who wants to start a family soon. If you know you want to be the CEO of your current company and that's your main priority, you'd be wasting your time and your potential love interest's time by starting a romantic relationship now, unless he or she is willing to wait. You can always call them back in a year or two and see if they want to date again. From my experience, when one person wants something totally different than the other person does, negative things start to surface, like resentment, anger, and hurt feelings.

One of my co-workers, Tony, was dating a woman for almost a year. From the beginning of their relationship, they always had fights about the fact that he didn't want to get more serious. Recently, he came into work and told me that they broke up. Here's how the conversation went down.

> Me: "Dude, what happened?"
> Tony: "She was bugging, yo. Wanted to settle down and was getting on me for working too much. That's my money, ya know?"
> Me: "I feel you, but hey. Let me ask you something. When you guys met for the first time, did you have, like, a list in your head?"
> Tony: "Huh?"
> Me: "Criteria, qualities that you can't live without."

Tony: "Not really. She was cute and that's what mattered, you feel me?"

Me: "Has she always wanted to settle down and go fast?"

Tony: "Oh yeah, from day one she's been on me about moving in and quitting my job."

Me: "Dude, that's why you need a woman who doesn't give you deadlines."

Tony: "That would have helped for sure. Dang, Lauren, I could have saved a year!"

Me: "I don't know about all that, but you could have saved something."

Tony definitely could have helped himself by having a Top 5 List. As a young person, it's especially important to be clear about the things that you need in a dating partner to avoid situations like Tony's.

William's #2: Intelligent

I like women who have clarity in their eyes, know what they like, can converse on many levels, and know how to engage their man. She has to have an air of confidence, sophistication, and voluptuous body parts to get by my initial screen. But I usually hit the *go* button when I detect a certain level of intelligence. Conversely, as a middle-aged man, I know that beauty and sexuality are not enough to compensate for a lack of smarts.

Shortly after college, I met and dated an attractive lady who was a gifted writer. We spent many evenings reading her poetry and other literary passages. It was hot listening to many of them, and we also had great discussions on their message. Her views always helped me see things differently, and her energy got my juices flowing. I realized the importance of being in a relationship with someone who mentally engages you and then can touch your intimate hot buttons. Wow. Unfortunately, we drifted apart after college graduation. She wanted to go into secondary education in

Detroit, and I was committed to becoming a corporate superstar while living in Cincinnati.

An intelligent person who is attracted to you is a powerful energy force. They are curious, aggressive, and not willing to accept B.S. Their perceptions and attention to detail are stimulating. Their awareness of the world keeps you on your toes, and there is no way for you to get lazy and mediocre. They push and encourage you. They drive you to stay current, relevant, and improve.

> - W -
> Remember, looks always go away.

I ignored the intelligence quality for a long time. Often a quick encounter with a beautiful and/or party person was satisfactory. But that was in my twenties and early thirties. As I grew older, I found the mornings after these dates left me unfulfilled. At some point, I realized that my radar always went up when the other person was a good conversationalist and thought-provoking. To me, the worst date in the world is being with a dummy, no matter how fly she is.

Lauren's #3: Stable

Will all of the stable peeps put their hands up?

There are a lot of people, particularly of a young age, who deal with frequent changes in their lives that may cause stress and a constant feeling of being unsettled. This can come in various forms: problems with paying rent, constantly moving, not being able to keep a job, or always getting into trouble. We all know someone like this, whether it's a family member, a friend, or an ex-lover. Being around them is never smooth sailing or easy since there's always an issue popping up in their life.

I was recently asked out by a nice, attractive, and smart woman. She sent me a message on Facebook and invited me to a dance performance that she was doing. I accepted and looked forward to it the rest of the week.

After the show, she came over to me with her friends and I couldn't tell by her body language if she was interested. So, I went home shortly afterward and asked—via text—if she was interested in dating. The answer I got was "I'm not opposed to it, but things are in transition. I like you. It's just, career stuff, moving to New York, and my living

> **- W -**
> When you've got a lady or a man who blows you away, there's no way you wouldn't move with your Boo or do long distance. Your heart wouldn't allow it.

situation are unclear at the moment. I'm hoping to move back to California in three years after I move this summer."

This girl is awesome, but not for me. When things are unstable in someone's life, that chaos will only be brought into yours. Take my advice and simply be friends until the tides have changed.

Start with a list of as many qualities as you can, then cut them down to the essentials.

William's #3: Enjoyable Company

For middle-aged folks, fun means *enjoyable.* Here is the tricky part for me. I don't like silly stuff and nothing-talk. You don't have to be a ball of intensity, but any time spent on a date needs to bring two people closer together.

> **- W -**
> No matter what age you are, FUN must always be in the dating equation. If it isn't there, do something different on your dates or be real about the fact that it may not work.

And the fun has to come from the personas within each person. You cannot rely on the event you are attending, a great movie, or a wonderful dinner to make your evening enjoyable. These things are simply supplementary, making the date even more fun. So, when I was single, I always asked myself, *Can I have fun with this person doing something simple and low-key? Can I be myself?* Typically, a Ladies' Man or Playa can spice it up with ease. The Good Guys have to be careful not to get boring. Fellas, do you have game?

In my thirties, I dated a stunning Cajun lady from New Orleans. I always got mesmerized by her green eyes, long black hair, J-Lo body, and perfect caramel complexion. We dined in romantic places and ended the evenings in steamy intimacy. After a few of these dates, I started to realize that something was missing. We didn't connect on almost anything. Conversations at dinner were mostly staring, exchanging polite pleasantries about our day, and focusing on the meal. I was captivated by her looks and the romantic evening conclusions.

Enjoyable means you can have a great date as two people, one-on-one. Stimulating conversation is the main ingredient in creating a connection. No matter the date venue, the personal connection should be the main driver and you must enjoy each other's company.

Let's Break It Down
Hump Phase

Our Top 5 Lists have a *Hump Phase.* Points #1–3 are viewed as *necessary* to take someone on a date. These qualities can deliver an active dating life with good benefits. However, **points #4 and 5** are characteristics we *expect* in order to have the potential for a long-term, more committed relationship. In other words, to get the **Homerun Companion** in your camp, the person you are attracted to **must hit all of your Top 5.**

Lauren's #4: Drama-Free

There's nothing worse than being around someone who makes you feel like you're on pins and needles all the time. You never know what they're going to say or do, but you know it won't be good. As if life doesn't already throw enough twists and turns, these folks throw a huge boulder in the road, causing you and everyone else in their lives to drive right off the cliff. Fortunately, most of us learn from the crash and try hard to stay away from these kinds of peeps.

When you're attracted to that special somebody, drama can be sexy and exciting. "Gurl, he has a short temper, but it's kind of hot when he gets all loud." "She never really calls me back, but I like a challenge." These are major issues, yet most of us overlook them or get off on them. I can relate to that. It's not easy to see when we're addicted to this unhealthy dance. Or we see how bad it is, but we like it so much that we continue feeding the chaos. Fine, but don't expect a long-lasting and stress-free relationship to develop out of it.

It's definitely a good idea to consider going the route of peace and consistency instead of instability and O-M-G. When I meet a woman who is very beautiful, but not good for me, I always ask myself this question:

Would I rather sip a piña colada on the beach or be in the middle of a tornado?

That's kind of how it is when you're dating a guy or gal who is nothing but drama. You won't ever truly feel safe or like you have a solid foundation. This feeling of drama can be a wide range of things, from always being negative to initiating fights to never having stability. Regardless of which one it is, it only brings you down.

I dated a stripper not too long ago. She was a nice person and, as you can imagine, had a bangin' body. I was really feelin' her and told myself: *I can learn to deal with this. She's a nice person.* And, at first, the dancing didn't bother me until, after a few months of dating, I started to see some things I wasn't down with, like how she drank a lot. Or how she liked to hang out with other strippers and go to other clubs with them. When we hung out, she often seemed hungover or not present at all. Sure, she had some amazing qualities, but the stress and drama in her life only added more to mine. Before I knew it, I was taking time out of my day to make sure she was okay. I would wonder if she made it home okay or had anyone bother her at the club. It took me a long time to get past her nice body and our sexual chemistry to be able to let go, but when I did, it felt like a big weight had been lifted off my shoulders. I'll take a piña colada for sure.

***Consistency is sexy. It means you can count on someone to
be who they are day in and day out.***

William's #4: Shared Values

Now it's getting serious. Mature people usually don't have
the patience to socialize with individuals who aren't on the
same wavelength that they are.

The most common example relates to family—for
example, you are super involved
with your children, and your
boyfriend/girlfriend has always
been single, carefree, and
insensitive about family ties. Not a
good picture. Or you are in a very

> - **W** -
> Sometimes a lack of passion in
> life can be a bigger turnoff than
> bad breath or not showering for
> a few days. You can't force
> passion into someone, but you
> can give 'em soap.

demanding job, sometimes working crazy hours, but your
date is a pure nine-to-five person, mostly detached from his
or her career, and gets impatient with your work
distractions. Again, not a good picture.

Other values that I consider important are honesty,
sensitivity, religious beliefs, and work ethic. Whatever is on
your list, stick by it. Compromises here are a killer.

You cannot go against your values and core beliefs to
become something you are not. In turn, the other person
cannot either. After that first encounter, you should test your
date and find out where they stand on your important issues.
If they don't give you the answers you want, drop them. I
don't mean to sound harsh, but you can't waste time on an
individual who plays games or isn't on the same level.

Lauren's #5: Passionate

I was watching Dr. Phil the other day on an episode of *Oprah*
discussing how many people don't recognize they're
depressed until they've experienced happiness. In this
particular case, he was referring to those of us who went to
work every day, did what was asked of us, and clocked out,
year after year. It wasn't until they changed direction in life
that they felt good, like things just fit into place.

I immediately understood what he was saying, probably because I've been there—ya know, just going through the motions and not enjoying most areas of my life. When you're not satisfied in one area of your life, it tends to spread around to others.

Things started to turn around for me when I took a huge chance and moved to New York to attend film school. For me and my family, this was a big deal. I had never lived anywhere but California and had absolutely no family in the Big Apple. But I felt passionate about screenwriting and learning more about my craft. When I made the move, it was hard, but I felt motivated, inspired, and alive. I had never worked so hard before in my life, and I loved it. My days were filled with films, writing, and classes. It was awesome, and having that experience made me value and respect passion. To this day, though I don't have my dream job (yet), I still feel the same way I did in New York because nothing can take away that joy I felt back then.

> - L -
> The stripper I dated had no strong motivation in life and that's exactly how she acted while we dated: never planned anything or put any major effort into making sweet gestures.

In my eyes, passionate peeps are the best ones to date. As a twenty-something, I want to be around someone who is motivated in her career or passion since, at this age, that's where most of our time goes. Plus, just being around driven individuals is not only inspiring, but also sexy. You don't have to worry about them falling apart or being too needy because they have their own thing going on and feel secure in what they do. Not only that, but you know if they're willing to do whatever it takes for their dreams in life, *he or she will go all out for you.* It's what my good friend calls the "I got your back" factor. No matter what, you're covered because that person will go to the end of the Earth for you. From my experience, a lack of motivation or passion in life creates other problems, like a lack of energy or desire to make an effort in the relationship.

William's #5: Passionate

I agree with Lauren on this one. It is important to date someone who is committed to something, sometimes called *fire in the belly*. The ideal date understands and appreciates who you are and is a cheerleader for the things you are pursuing, and you have the same support for their dreams.

Over the years, I was in relationships with people who did not fully understand or try to relate to my executive ambitions (my previous passion). As a corporate up-and-comer, I worked hard and rose fast. But there were lots of trips, long office

> **- W -**
> It's almost impossible to have a successful dating relationship if the person doesn't like what you do for a living or support your passion in life.

days, and business calls at home. The fruits of my labor provided me and my family with a wonderful lifestyle, but it also led to frequent ridicule and resentment from my partners. When this type of tension surrounds your passion, something has to go. It's not hard to guess the outcome.

When I started dating my future wife Jennifer, I was leaving the corporate world to become a professional golfer. This was a radical move—leaving a high-six-figure job to work up the ladder of professional golf. That was like Michael Jordan leaving basketball to pursue Major League Baseball. And we know how that ended. Not good. But Jennifer embraced my passion, ignoring the risks and naysayers and the huge income loss I incurred. She was my biggest cheerleader and confidant. Finally, one day, after dating for several years, I realized Jennifer hit my entire Top 5 List. I never had that with a person I dated or in my previous marriage. Soon after I came to this revelation, we tied the knot.

A few years after we were married, Jennifer wanted to leave her corporate position and start a new business. We carefully analyzed several options and chose to open a high-end pet resort. She loved animals and considered this to be her lifelong dream. I could see her passion and decided to give her my one hundred percent unconditional support. Today, we own and operate one of the most successful pet resorts in the country.

Middle-aged people can often lose their passion because it seems too risky or unconventional. They don't want people to talk about them. So, they program themselves to do predictable things. Ask yourself: *Does my life contain something to be passionate about?*

Passion gets you up in the morning, it keeps you young and happy, and it makes you interesting. My dates needed to appreciate passion, be supportive, and have a passion about something. A lack of passion is not attractive.

What's on Your List?

We know our lists are small and might be excluding other characteristics that you feel are extremely important, which is why we encourage you to make your own. In fact, you may already have an idea of what's on your Top 5 List from prior dating experience. Awesome. Maybe we gave you some ideas from this chapter. Regardless, we strongly

> **- W -**
> We know this isn't the most fun thing to do, but just buckle down and do it. This will help you in the long run.

recommend that you write down your top choices. It's a great reminder, and you'll see just how much you tend to stray from your list. In the box below, write down your Top 5 qualities.

My Top 5 List

1) _____

2) _____

3) _____

4) _____

5) _____

We encourage you to print this out and post it on your refrigerator or somewhere you can view it on a regular basis. And if your friends hate on you or give you a hard time, just ignore them. You'll get the last laugh as they remain single and you find your perfect match.

By focusing on what you want, the chances of attracting it increase.

Beware of These Breeds

Although we agree that most people are worthy of at least one date, some can be ruled out before you even pull out that Top 5 List.

Allow us to break it down.

1. *Bad Boys/Bad Girls*
You don't stand a chance at finding long-term love if you're always chasing the *bad* types, no matter how good it feels at the time. Don't pretend you don't know the warning signs. That certain sparkle and unpredictable nature. The excitement you feel in their rambling and restless minds. Their actions aren't controlled by anything so mundane as values, political correctness, or respect for others. There's something dangerous and daring in everything they do. Gunshots may get fired or you may end up getting robbed— who knows? Remember, though, when you saddle up it's always on their terms. They may make promises or appear to be good, but, behind your back, you can't trust them for a second.

2. *Known Playas*
It's never a good thing when you're asking a friend about someone cute and she says, "Oh, he's cool. Sleeps with every girl he can, but I heard he's nice."

Not hot.

When you're gold, peeps like this have no right to even show up on your radar, unless you want to be with a

Quick Hit. They are only out to hit-it-and-quit-it—not just with you, but everyone else on the block, too. If you dare to consider a Known Playa as a serious dating candidate, prepare to get hurt.

3. *Homeless (or close enough to it)*
Let's say you're interested in a guy you always run into at the coffee shop. He's cute and has great eyes and an awesome body. So, you finally start a conversation with him and it goes something like this:

> You: "Hey, how are you?"
> Guy: "Hi. Good, just buying this Thai latte I can't afford."
> You: "I love those."
> Guy: "Yeah, me, too. Wonder why it went up ten cents this week."
> You: "Uh, okay. So, you live around here?"
> Guy: "Kind of. I just got kicked out of my place, so I'm crashing where I can."
> You: "Bummer. For how long?"
> Guy: "Who knows? I'm not thinking about it."

The conversation should definitely end at this point. Forget telling him your name. You two are at completely different stages in your life. Maybe once he has an apartment, a job, and enough money

> - W -
> Going through hard times is understandable, but that's not your problem. Let the storm pass and then make your move.

to buy a latte, you can consider busting out your Top 5 List. Until then, keep it nicely tucked inside your pocket and jet out the door.

4. *Freshly Out of Rehab*
Do we even need to say anything? Come on.

5. *Noncommittal*

Lauren: I know a few men like this from my job—a great catch who would make an awesome partner, but not at this time, because they don't want to be held down.

One of the fellas I work with loves hitting on women and asking them out on dates. These women go and start falling for him within a month's time. Little do they know that he has no plans to be in a relationship—that is, until they ask him to settle down and he says, "Naw, I got too much going on right now."

6. *Sex Addicts*

Russell Brand seems like an awesome guy, but let's get real— he's probably going to cheat on Katy Perry down the road just like Eric Benét did on Halle Berry. Once a sex addict, always a sex addict.

Let's Break It Down
Ask questions

Before using your Top 5 List on someone, it's critical to find out if both of you want the same kind of dating situation. "Are you looking to date?" "Do you want to eventually be in a relationship?" "Is hooking up your main priority?" These are the kinds of questions that you shouldn't feel uncomfortable asking, because if you're not on the same page, then there's *no point in using your Top 5 List*. Only use it on peeps who match up with your romantic needs.

Using the List: Online Dating

Now's the perfect time to join a few dating websites with your Top 5 List snuggled next to you. Here are some things to look out for as you surf through profiles.

➤ Don't click on a profile in which the person is drunk, kissing someone, or doing something offensive. This is always a bad sign and gives off the impression that you're dealing with a Not Serious. First impressions are everything, and if they want to present themselves in that way, what is that saying? **Lauren**: I have been through a handful of these and they never had a positive outcome. Don't get sucked in because they're hot.

➢ Join a credible, popular dating website. There's a lot of clutter and whack options out there. So, make sure to research all of them by using Google or another good search engine. It won't take long to find the ones that have a high success rate and a good reputation, such as Match.com or eHarmony.

➢ If they take more than a day to respond, move on ASAP.
Lauren: A woman emailed me recently about going out for drinks. I responded within a few hours saying, "I'm down. Let me know." A day went by and she still hadn't responded. So I didn't reach out after that. If she couldn't respond to a simple question within a day's time, she'd probably act the same way in a relationship.

➢ After contact has been made, set up a date within a week. It's easy to become a forgotten email or last on the list when you're only known for a profile picture. Take advantage of their attention and quickly make a time to hang out.

➢ It's all about the *headline.* Don't underestimate the power of a few words. While you're creating a profile on a dating website, sixty percent of your time should go to coming up with a unique headline. Use every opportunity you have to stand out and show your personality.

➢ Don't fall in love with a photograph. Trust us when we say a person can look completely different face-to-face than they do online. Maybe the picture that you saw was from three years ago before they gained forty pounds. Or let's say their entire body has tattoos and you aren't okay with that. Wait until you meet before getting excited.

➢ Read *introductions.* This is important because it's one of the first impressions they make. Based on what we've seen, most peeps are either what we call a **Lazy** or an ***I Ain't Playin' Around***. A Lazy will write only one or two sentences, like "My friends made me join this website, so this is really just an experiment." An I Ain't Playin' Around will throw down several detailed paragraphs about who they are and what they're looking for in a dating candidate.

➢ Pay money. It's too easy to sign up for a dating website and forget all about it. By paying a monthly fee, there's more of an investment and the quality tends to be better. Also, to be real, peeps who are serious about finding love don't mind spending a few hundred dollars.
Lauren: For those of you in your twenties or struggling to pay rent, don't worry. A lot of dating websites have a monthly payment plan so you only have to fork up $30 or $40 a month. That's equal to three or four drinks at a bar. You can do it.

➢ *Sign on* at least three times a week. There's nothing worse than clicking on a profile that says "Active within three months." If you slack on checking up on your page, don't throw a fit when you see a blown opportunity with someone awesome who tried to reach out to you.

➢ Avoid emotions. "I really like you." "There's obviously a strong connection between us." "You may be The One." If these words are coming out of your fingers before seeing each other in person, turn off your laptop and don't type another sentence until you meet.

➢ Be as open as possible. On many dating websites, you fill out detailed information about yourself: weight, height, income, religious background, age, and so forth. We suggest revealing as much as you can so that you don't waste time or give off the wrong impression. You don't want to increase the chances of rejection or bad surprises because you were too private.

➢ Use pictures to show your world. If you're a family-oriented woman who is career-focused, show this using photographs. This is your chance to tell a story and reveal as much as you can in a short period of time. ***Make every click matter.***

➢ Avoid obsession. You have to keep moving around. Sure, there may be one person in particular who really catches your eye, but you can't put your eggs in one basket. Let that guy or gal know you're interested and then see what happens.

Don't Budge
Once you have your Top 5 List, don't budge. You deserve to be one hundred percent happy with the person you choose to date. Plus, when you deviate from your list, life tends to be harder. You'll start wasting time, put yourself in a vulnerable position to get hurt, and be extremely distracted from your passion in life or career.

This is easier said than done—especially when you're looking at a sexy guy or gal in front of you. Who would turn that down? *You.* There will always be someone else who will come along and fit your needs *in addition* to being very attractive. You have to believe it to see it, though.

Chapter Summary

William's Old School Wisdom	Lauren's New School Wisdom
Make your Top 5 List and carry it in your wallet or purse for frequent reminders.	Don't forget that dating should be fun, and the people you hang around should be fun, too.
Quickly rate potential dates early in the encounter. (Example: If she covers only the first two on your list, it's probably a Quick Hit.)	Stay positive and expect that you'll attract an amazing individual. Like attracts like.
Don't try to change your values and passions to be with someone. You'll be unhappy in the end.	Go out with good friends to a club so they can keep you away from the wrong types when you're distracted by his or her looks or charm.
Attend special events and gatherings that have purpose. Check out the ladies. Female activists have a lot of intellectual and seductive qualities.	Use online dating, and make sure you check the site on a consistent basis.

How to Flirt on Facebook

➢ Suggest hanging out in response to a status update. If he's talking about wanting a burger from In-N-Out, then you can reply, "I'm hungry. When are we going?" It's a cute way to invite yourself, and if he's interested; you'll be grubbing soon.

➢ "Like" when it matters. If she's going to the store to pick up a gallon of milk, there's no need to waste a "like" on that. However, if homegirl is ecstatic about the opening of her new film or landing a new client, click that button until your fingers go numb.

➢ Respond to their status updates on a consistent basis. ***Notification is motivation.*** If your crush is always being alerted to something you've said, there's a good chance he or she will also feel motivated to drop you a line back.

➢ Comment on *sexy* pictures. See some nice legs or appreciate the way he looks in his Timberlands? Say it. "Your legs look great in that dress." "Love how sexy you look in those T's." Directness works.

➢ Who doesn't love a good poke? Use the "poke" button, and if you get poked back, then you have it in the bag. Don't let things dwindle, though. Send an email and ask for a date as a way to follow up and seal the deal.

➢ Invite them to events you're throwing or attending. Definitely don't go over two invites a week. If the consistent response is "not attending" or "maybe," then it's probably best to stop reaching out.

➢ Instant message **no more than twice a week**. The point is to stay on their radar. Even if the conversation is short, you won't be forgotten.

➢ Only flirt with one person a time. Don't become a **Facebook Ho** by leaving flirtatious posts on various profiles. Since everything you say is public, word will spread fast and you won't be taken seriously.

How *NOT* to Flirt on Facebook

Every day there are sad stories of people being *unfriended* for all kinds of reasons. We don't want you to be one of those tragedies.

> ➢ ***Comment-a-holic.*** You leave a variety of long and short passages on most—if not all—of your crush's status updates. Plus, you like to write daily posts with funny jokes or a cute article you read. So not cool or sexy.

> ➢ Using *every* opportunity as a way to hang out. If their status updates often refer to "hanging out at home" or "spending time with family," this isn't a chance for you to invite yourself over.

> ➢ Always referring to your crush in status updates. That's so not sexy and definitely crosses boundaries.

> ➢ Instant messaging too much. If they're on four or five times a day, don't always pop-up their spot.

> ➢ Suggest that they add your close friends and family members. Sure, you want to be an open book, but your momma doesn't need to be the one holding it.

> ➢ ***Over-winking.*** If you're the only one on the wink train, stop and get off.

> ➢ Making short videos for them. It's cool for friends to send each other video greetings, but you're still in the *I-don't-know-you* phase. Put the camera down.

3.
Caution
Flags

If you lived next door to an ex-convict, you'd double lock your doors at night just to be safe. So, why not treat your heart the same way?

Let's assume that you are in the initial phase of seeing someone. You know, meandering through the first date or two, texting, phone calls, and so forth. Yeah, it can be uncomfortable going through the *getting-to-know-you* steps, but it's crucial. Equally important is not letting little differences get in the way. The things you notice might be *different-different* and not *different-bad*, like she's a vegetarian and you're not, you have differing tastes in movies, or he prefers CNN to ESPN. These differences can be viewed as opportunities for growth, not necessarily grounds for elimination.

Also, at this stage in the game, you know how to be more visible and have a better idea of what you're looking for in Mr. or Ms. Right. You may have met someone or have a pocketful of numbers from potential dating candidates. Perhaps, you're even thinking

> **- W -**
> A disconnection isn't always bad. Sometimes, it's a matter of learning how to communicate better and adjusting to the other person's needs.

that you found The One, but feel like something just isn't clicking. For whatever reason, there's a disconnection between you guys and you're one text message away from tripping out.

The things that aren't clicking are what we call *Caution Flags*, which are not to be ignored. You have to take a long look at these in order to see whether or not there's potential for a dating relationship. You've just arrived at first base, but still have a ways to go before reaching home plate. Right now, it's about looking more closely at the person you're thinking of being with and getting real in terms of what you can and cannot deal with. Perhaps, it's a sloppy appearance or a short temper. Finding a way to see Caution Flags is essential to dating successfully, just like knowing what each light means when you're driving on a strange highway.

Red = Stop   **Yellow** = Caution   **Green** = Go

It sounds easy, and it's a breeze to remember when we're driving a car (remember, you had to pass a driver's test to get your license, and you know the laws). So most of us automatically know to stop at a red light or double check when it's green to make sure we don't get blindsided. It's second nature. We even know when to slow down as green turns to yellow. Yellow means caution. Thus, you have to think about changing your speed and your intentions to go, proceeding slowly, or stopping entirely.

Why is it that when we land on the dating scene, we sometimes ignore visible Caution Flags? Caution Flags can be subtle. Early in the game, they can be explained away or even ignored because the sparks are still flying and your juices are flowing. When you meet someone you think is interesting, but has some unique tendencies or behaviors, ask yourself these questions:

- Do these things make me feel uncomfortable?
- Do they keep me off balance?
- Are they funny or weird?
- Is this something I can live with forever?
- Am I feeling good in my heart?
- Is this an indication of an issue that can get bigger and uglier down the road?

The big message here is: Pay attention to your gut feelings and intuition.

We've each compiled a list of Caution Flags for you to watch for in a love interest. These are No-Nos to look out for on a superficial level, whether you're twenty or fifty-five years old. No doubt, it's your decision to take these into account and decide what to do after that, but having the knowledge will bring you closer to your goal in finding the right partner.

LAUREN'S #1

TEXTAHOLIC

This one is nonnegotiable. If you're on a date and he keeps looking at his cell phone, texting, or receiving calls after you've expressed not liking it, then you're better off bouncing. I wouldn't say get up and leave, because we all gotta eat. However, after finishing your meal, think of a quick excuse to end the date soon. It's one thing to text once or twice, but not throughout the entire date.

I went on a date a few years ago with an attractive girl. We went to a pool hall and flirted for the first hour of our date. Things were going well until she started checking her cell phone and texting between each shot. I wasn't into it, but decided to see if she'd stop after a few minutes. Luckily, she did—but only for about an hour. I finally said something and she promised to stop. Later, we went back to my place and she got up to use the restroom—and took her purse with her. I thought, *that's strange, but hey, this is New York.* After ten minutes went by, I knew something wasn't right. I knocked on the door to check on her and could hear her typing away on her cell phone. She was texting on the toilet!

That experience made me realize that I deserve to be respected and valued by every person in my life. Texting in front of someone while you're together is rude and disrespectful. If that's happening to you (or has), you deserve better. To be real, there are many folks who will gladly keep their attention on you for a night, which is what you deserve. It's not cool to take your attention off of the person you're face-to-face with and give it to a plastic device.

Keep in mind that Caution Flags focus on the beginning stages of dating, not a relationship. In the latter case, it's to be expected that you need to be on the phone sometimes for business, personal reasons, and so forth.

WILLIAM'S #1

SINGLE PARENT WITH RESTRICTIONS

As a single dad, I thought it would be tricky to see success on the dating scene. Surprisingly, a lot of ladies were drawn to an attractive, professional guy raising one of his kids alone. They would come over with toys, books, and often jumped into the flow of fixing dinner. I enjoyed their sensitivity, care, and patience with my situation. They were not turned off by my restricted time demands due to such things as work, little league games, and school meetings. Generally speaking, women handle this situation better than men. Still, I felt fortunate.

> - W -
> Parents: Getting a babysitter on a regular basis so you can date doesn't mean you're not a good parent. You deserve to have a break every now and then.

As a contrast, I had several single buddies who couldn't date single moms. Guys in general seem to be frightened off by ladies with parental obligations. Why? Guys are more self-centered. Yes, I said it fellas. Guys want their dates to be available for fun events, travel, and romantic interludes. Frequently turning down opportunities or being overly preoccupied with the kids' activities must be matched with a quality effort to show the guy that she can balance both. I didn't say it was fair, but guys are more insecure. Restrictions can be managed, but single parents must be able to "multitask."

Don't forget, children have the ability to ambush great date activities. You might call home in the middle of dinner to find out your kids are fighting with the babysitter or little Johnny fell and had to go to the emergency room for a broken arm. Plans to slip in the back door with your Boo and go upstairs for a happy ending are foiled by little Susie standing at the stairs in her PJs saying, "Hi Mommie, are you going to read me a story tonight?" Oh yeah, patience is important!

Two single parents trying to date each other is the hardest match. The complications go up exponentially, particularly if the children are really young. Sure, one person may have help from family or a great daycare center. Eventually, however, those options wear thin; any good parent will want to spend time with their child on a frequent basis. Frankly speaking, there's only so much time and energy you have left for a new Boo after work and hanging with little Johnny. Don't go into this type of dating relationship unless the other person is irresistible and hits everything on your Top 5 List.

LAUREN'S #2

DRESSED NOT TO IMPRESS

Pajamas on in public.
Wearing casual clothes at an upscale dinner.
Baggy attire.
Tennis shoes at the club.

These are only a few examples of dressing whack. There's no excuse nowadays to look torn up or like you just came from off the street.

It's important to feel confident about the person you're dating, but hard to do if they dress inappropriately. This can range from always wearing too much makeup to going out in public with pajamas on to keeping their

> **- L -**
> If you're at a loss with regard to shopping for cute clothes, ask a stylish friend to help you. My roommate, Glenn, took me shopping after I lost weight and still does to this day.

hair messy. There are people out there who don't care about these things, which is okay. However, most peeps won't feel comfortable or be accepting of an individual who looks unkempt and dirty. If you're in this situation, consider asking yourself why you're choosing to date someone who pays so little attention to the way they look. If you're on the fence about someone like this, I would consider grabbing the remote and pausing. You can definitely make a suggestion to him or her about dressing better, but that can come off as trying to change who they are, which rarely goes well. You're probably better off moving on or accepting who they are at this time.

When I was overweight, I dressed in baggy clothes and never wore makeup or did anything to add a nice touch to my appearance. I didn't feel good about myself and that was obvious by the way I dressed. And when I got hit on, it was by peeps who didn't have a nice or neat look. Now that I feel more confident, I take pride in what I wear and how I present myself to the world. I also attract other peeps who feel the same way on the inside and take pride in their image.

When you're dealing with someone who is dirty, it takes away from being able to neck comfortably.

WILLIAM'S #2

OVERDONE APPEARANCE

Simply stated, too much of anything is a turnoff. For me, it used to be women with too much makeup and long fingernails. Then it went to big hair and cosmetic surgery. That said, I have no problem with people improving their looks or getting things fixed to be healthier. But remember Michael Jackson and what he did to his body. It went from one change to a handful over many years.

Often, when someone focuses too much on their appearance, there is some deep-seated insecurity they are concealing or trying to overcome. What is this person trying to project or hide? This is what would enter my mind when I dated someone like this.

A buddy of mine dated a lady from Los Angeles who was stunning and very personable. Her hair was big and perfectly styled; she was always dressed in "after six" attire. In contrast, he was more down to earth and dressed accordingly. After dating for about

> **- W -**
> "After six" attire is for the mature and sexy. It may be a short skirt for a lady and a chest-hair-showin' button-down for a man.

six months, I noticed her wearing more jeans and other more leisurely clothing. It was obvious that she realized her approach was over the top and toned it down a bit. I give her credit for a willingness to realistically look in the mirror.

It's okay to date a person with an over-the-top appearance, but they need to have enough of your Top 5 qualities to give it a chance. If they are perceptive enough, they will adjust. If he or she doesn't pick up on your discomfort, then you can choose to say something. However, keep in mind that you're in the beginning stages of dating, not in a relationship. You don't have to overly communicate or feel any obligation to continue dating him or her.

LAUREN'S #3

FUNKY SMELL

Well, this is a tough one. Some folks just sweat a lot and have bad natural body odor. This can be helped by deodorant, but it doesn't make the smell fully go away. This is different than smelling bad due to rarely, or never, taking a shower or having bad hygiene. To be real, though, it doesn't matter where the funk originates. If it's there, it's there. You may find that you can live with it, but if you can't, then peace out.

In college, I was interested in dating this woman with dreads and a gorgeous smile. She was very sweet and a great listener. The only thing was that she rarely showered and smelled bad as a result. She chose to not shower due to her moral beliefs about the environment. I remember her being in a room with our friends and having to open all of the windows because the stench was so strong. We would flirt, laugh, and have fun together. But things never went to the next level because I was so uncomfortable with her body odor, and there was no way I was going to tell her to change it. She probably sensed my discomfort as well.

Peeps are more intuitive than we think. Chances are, before you say what's on your mind, they know what's coming.

WILLIAM'S #3

LONG DISTANCE

It seems like all of my best dating relationships had a distance issue. I can't explain it, but the ladies I remember most required travel. It's probably one of the reasons I used to sing Marvin Gaye's "Distant Lover" all the time.

A few years back, I dated a wonderful lady I'll call Sandra. She had the natural genes. Sandra had a great hourglass shape with wide shoulders, big chest, and killer hips. She was probably fifteen pounds overweight, but carried it in a way that made you want to see more. To top it off, she wore a closely cut natural hairdo, a little makeup around the eyes, and a deep, glossy lipstick. She was comfortable in her own skin and confident around men. She worked for an insurance company in the Northeast and I lived in the Midwest. As much as I wanted this relationship to work, we fell short. There was too much career ambition between us and too much sexuality to save up for weekend encounters once a month. We both wanted to be in a committed relationship, but we were selfish about our careers. In the end, the distance issue was the straw that broke the camel's back.

> - W -
> If you're looking for a fling, a flight attendant is perfect. They don't put any pressure on you due to their schedule, plus they always have stories to tell about places they've traveled.

There was also the beautiful and engaging flight attendant. On my way back to Michigan from a business trip, I connected with Ann while she was doing her super service at 40,000 feet in the friendly skies. We spent the next few weeks having many long-distance telephone calls. This was later mixed with a few layovers while she was passing through on working flights.

Ann was stunning. She had the "It Factor" supreme. Our relationship developed at warp speed. After a few months of crazy intensity, we were talking about moving in together. She requested to get her home base changed to a city close to me, but the airline company had a one-year wait list for transfers. So, after four months of long-distance calls, short weekend trips, and one-night layovers, we started to realize this was a tough way to date or have a relationship. We missed too many events, casual moments, and one-on-one growth time. We discussed her commuting from Michigan, but this increased her travel time significantly. Without much discussion, we subconsciously started to allow our jobs and other interests to pull us apart. The calls and hangouts eventually stopped without a major announcement of our intent. What I learned from that was: a) distance is not good for long-term dating and b) decisions must be made sooner versus later.

Being selfish isn't a bad thing. You come first before any man or woman (unless we're talking about your kid).

LAUREN'S #4

LANGUAGE BARRIER

> - L -
> A strong language barrier might have worked in *Love Actually*, but not in real life.

One time I met a Swedish woman who was visiting California from out of town at a local bar in Hollywood. She was nice, charming, and sexy. Plus, her face and body were on point. The only thing I had an issue with was her words. Her accent was so thick that I had to always ask, "What did you say?" This wasn't a deal breaker for me, which is why we continued hanging out. However, after a short time, it ended. Our poor verbal communication was too much of an issue. In the end, I felt frustrated and annoyed by the fact that we couldn't get on the same page except when we kissed.

Not being able to comprehend what someone is saying, especially your love interest, is a big deal. This can range from poor grammar to not knowing a certain language. By no means am I advising you to just run away. But take a hard, long look at things and ask yourself if you can deal with it. Can you go out in public or with your friends and not feel embarrassed or defensive that someone will make fun of your date? Are you willing to constantly repeat yourself each

> **- W -**
> Chances are, if you met The One, you'd probably make the effort to overcome these hurdles.

and every day without getting angry, resentful, or aggravated? I felt very bad that I couldn't deal with it, but I knew that ending things was the best thing to do before it got serious. After all, she deserves to be with someone who will appreciate the way she communicates, just like I do.

Let's Break It Down
Be clear

William: Since you're beginning to date and ask people out, it's important to be very clear about your intention. Let's say you're on the phone about to ask a guy or girl out. Avoid saying, "Let's hang out" or "We gotta catch up, man." Be clear. How? By expressing your true feelings: "I really want to see you—when are you available for drinks?" In other words, skip the **blurriness**. The worst scenario is having that person hang up the phone wondering if you like him or her at all.

WILLIAM'S #4

FRIENDS WITH AN EX

I never understood a woman telling me that her ex-boyfriend is now a good friend. What? You can't find other friends who can do the same things? I'm not down with that. No. In most cases, these are exes with *benefits.* Intimate benefits.

Sometimes the person is simply still getting over the relationship mentally. Guys are notorious for letting the relationship down slowly and hanging on to get these perks until she either gets sick and tired of our B.S. or finds a new fella. I've definitely been there, and it isn't easy to walk away when you have great physical chemistry. Plus, in most cases, it isn't only about that. There is usually some type of emotional connection that still lingers.

These situations are iffy. As the new person on the scene, you might get her to terminate the "friendship." But it depends on all of the other aspects of your relationship being right. Is it worth fighting for? I'd say no since you're just starting to date. If she or he is more interested in sleeping with an old flame, then you should let that be. You've got bigger and better things to do, like find someone who turns down the leftovers.

LAUREN'S #5

TOO FAKE

I once dated a woman with fake breasts, and it was awesome.

Fake isn't always bad. Let's be real, Pamela Anderson and Dolly Parton look great. You won't hear me complain about things that aren't natural, particularly if they look awesome. However, if the fakeness doesn't fit into their look or makes their appearance worse, then things may become challenging.

> - L -
> It's totally cool if your type is a woman with fake lips or a guy with a spray tan. Just don't complain if it turns into an obsession. You knew what you were getting into.

I think the larger issue is if a lot of things aren't natural, what does that say about how the person feels about himself or herself? Are they trying to completely cover up and change who they are? I would be cautious about these peeps. In the past, I've dated people who were obsessed with superficial things; it's a challenge to establish intimacy with a man or a woman so focused on the outside. A relationship without intimacy, vulnerability, and connection is one that doesn't last long.

WILLIAM'S #5

LACK OF GRATITUDE

Feedback is a powerful thing. When I considered someone to be special, I always wanted to do special things for them.

Keeping score is not always healthy, but, when dating, it is important to note who is doing the majority of the giving. Back in the day, when I was single, I loved when my date would say, "Let me cook for you next time," "I'm planning our next date," or "You are a special person for all you do." Even giving me a small gift to show her gratitude was fine. What didn't jive well was not showing appreciation for the effort I made, whether it was paying for dinner or planning a nice activity. Ungratefulness is a major turnoff, plus it sheds light on how a person will treat you down the road. If they aren't willing to pay for a $20 meal, then how will you be treated in a relationship with that individual? It's something to think about.

This can also relate to having a bad attitude. I never cared how sexy a woman was if she had a negative attitude. I'd rather be alone.

LAUREN'S #6

ALWAYS LATE

Being late to a date or to every outing is not cool. I gotta say, this is one of the biggest signs of disrespect in my eyes. You're probably just like me—working more than forty hours a week and exhausted each day. If you have free time, it's spent running errands, hanging with friends, or doing something for yourself. Time is valuable and there isn't much of it. So, when I take the time out to put on some makeup, buy a nice outfit, and drive over to meet a date, it's a big deal. I'm cutting into my sleep time and late nightcap before bed (ya'll know what I'm talkin' about). That's why I think it's important to have your own *grace period.* This is the amount of time you'll give your date to show up before you leave. For me, it's twenty minutes. For you it may be five minutes or an hour. The main thing is having one so that you won't spend the rest of your night waiting.

> - L -
> If you have difficulty being on time, buy a watch with a loud alarm clock and calendar that allows you to set reminders. Where there's a will, there's a way.

On a deeper level, consistently being late is a sign of immaturity and delusion. That person is so self-involved that they think only his or her schedule matters. Can you imagine what it would be like to be in a relationship with someone like this?

WILLIAM'S #6

ONLY AVAILABLE ON CERTAIN NIGHTS

Okay, so let's say you're dating a woman who is busy doing stuff on Saturday and Wednesday nights. She tells you this right up front when you meet. Or that she needs a lot of notice to go out. A good part of dating is spontaneity.

> **- W -**
> Getting your hair done or playing ball with the guys is not a good enough excuse to skip a date. Tell the salon to wait a day and your boys that you'll see them next week.

If she is free, honest, and willing, why does she need to plan so far in advance? Sometimes, the reasons are legit: job demands, family commitments, school, and the like. But you need to understand these real reasons for being unavailable. On the flip side, she could be a Playa with multiple guys in the mix. What is she not telling you? It's a Caution Flag. You need to address this tactfully and early in the game.

Being unavailable so early in the dating game may be a sign of what's to come down the road in a long-term relationship. Skip that.

LAUREN'S #7

"I LOVE YOU"

This is a tough one because most of us want to be loved. So why would we turn it away?

I've been in the position of dating an amazing woman who simply went too fast. It was hard to let go of her, but something didn't feel right about being told "I love you" in less than a month.

One night I was going for a walk and ran into a friend of mine. I hadn't seen him since he went home with a girl from the club we went to a few weeks ago. She was perfect for my friend—nice, single, cute, patient, and kind. So you can imagine that I was ready to hear even more good things when I asked, "How's it going with that girl you met at the club?"

My friend replied: "Terrible. She told me she loved me in an email like a week after we met and it freaked me out."

I didn't know what to say because I was so surprised. How can someone say "I love you" within such a short period of time, and in an email as opposed to face-to-face? Point is, the behavior isn't a good sign. It's too fast and too deep when things are at the most superficial level. Definitely consider bouncing if this happens to you.

WILLIAM'S #7

INSPIRES THAT "WHY ME?" FEELING

When your relationship seems one-sided for one reason or another, it's probably a good time to ask yourself: *Why me?*

On one of my business trips, I met an amazing lady named Marilyn. She was a server at an exclusive restaurant in Atlanta. She was a cutie pie with a great smile, soft manner, and knockout body. We got together on several of my trips to town and developed a fun relationship. I had no expectations for the future, but she grew on me. We enjoyed going to clubs, dancing, and hanging out. She also worked part-time as a fitness consultant for a local gym. As the weeks passed, I started to feel like Marilyn was holding something back. As it turned out, she was the single parent of a six-year-old boy. Due to her lifestyle, her young son was growing up as a latchkey kid. I tried to overlook Marilyn's parenting limitations, and became a good buddy to her son. Eventually, I couldn't get over the lack of attention she was giving him and the unlimited time she gave me on my visits. She focused on me and exposed me to many of her party-scene friends. I wasn't able to put the puzzle together. Something didn't feel right, so I called her and terminated the relationship without giving her my reasons. Not long afterward, I found out that Marilyn was still dating her son's dad, who happened to be a big drug dealer in town. So, why me? She obviously wanted a better life for herself and her son and wanted to get away from a bad environment. I was her ticket out. Close call.

LAUREN'S #8

ALWAYS UNEMPLOYED

Being unemployed for a year or so due to a rough economy is understandable. Refusing to work for months or years by choice isn't a good sign. Now, if the person is rich and doesn't have to work, that's different. But let's be real, there aren't many people like that out there.

When I went through a brief period of unemployment, I dated a woman who didn't work by choice, even though she needed to in order to pay bills. During that time, I started to be less active and found that I was allowing myself to be distracted since she was as well. As the days went by, I applied for only a few jobs. It was easy to waste time together.

> - L -
> Does the guy or gal you like inspire you to be a better person?

I always think that the person you're dating should inspire you to be a better person. In this case, it was the opposite for me. While I encouraged her to seek out work with me, she never did. As a result, I allowed myself to be brought down as well. It made me realize that I need to be with a person who is motivated and has a job.

WILLIAM'S #8

TOO SERIOUS

My best corporate years were in San Francisco and Los Angeles. While working in these environments, I dated many female executives. It had something to do with seeing attractive women in business attire during the day and in the buff at night. Not only were they usually attractive and smart, but they also were independent. Nothing got my adrenaline flowing more than getting into the minds of these ladies.

However, I did meet women who were too focused, too serious. These people are usually perfectionists who have a hard time laughing and finding value in humor. People who are too serious can be boring and old at heart. We used to call them stiff. You want a dating partner who can balance fun, seriousness, and all the in between. It's all about balance.

Chapter Summary

William's Old School Wisdom	Lauren's New School Wisdom
Your differences—culture, music, art—can be exciting new experiences to enrich your life. Embrace them with an open mind.	If they're only texting, it's time to run on home.
Character trumps cosmetics. If her appearance is over the top, but she is otherwise solid, give it time to evolve.	Follow your intuition, ladies. Guys, don't just follow your "man downstairs."
You can't fix ugly. If she takes you for granted and has a prima donna attitude, stop right there.	Run from the chaos. If a guy or girl is always mad about something or complaining about "da man" trying to sabotage them, bounce.
If it doesn't feel right, investigate. 50/50 chance there is an ex, financial problems, or something that could be a game changer.	Use Facebook to your advantage and read up on the person you're dating, but not too much. There is such a thing as Facebook stalkin'.
You can usually find some baggage on the other person. Be on the lookout. Are they simple Caution Flags or lethal	Consider walking away from anyone who has a kid or a few kids if you're just starting your adult life and

grenades?	career. You may not have time for that.

PEEPS ON A BUDGET
Date Ideas

Brought to you by Lauren

As everyone can tell by the shrinking of their wallets and purses, the economy is whack right now. Most young people (and some older) don't have a lot of money to spend on dating, particularly if they're going out on a regular basis. So, here's how you can save money and have a great time.

❖ **Museums.** You'll not only look smart by this suggestion, but also save some cash. Some museums don't charge an entry fee, just parking. Others have weekly or monthly free days or nights. If you take the bus, you're all set. It's romantic and informative.

❖ **Picnic on the beach.** You can't go wrong with this one.

❖ **Attend an intimate house party or gathering.** All you have to do is bring a bottle of cheap booze and you're guaranteed a great time.

❖ **Groupons.** Groupon.com is an awesome website where you can get daily coupons and special deals, such as a cheap massage or a three-course meal for only $40.

❖ **Cook at home.** I once dated a chef who cooked delicious meals for under $20.

❖ **Bike ride.** Rent a few bikes if you don't have them. This is a lot of fun and relieves stress.

❖ **Daytime movie/cheap theater.** I saw *Julie & Julia* for $4 with a woman I was dating and appreciated that only one other person was in the theater.

❖ **Free events in the park.** Sometimes, you can watch a free concert in the park or attend a cheap event. Check your local newspaper to catch these deals, especially during the summer.

❖ **Cafés.** There's usually no time limit, it's always a stress-free environment, and a cup of coffee shouldn't run you more than a few bucks. *Breakfast is always cheaper than dinner.*

PEEPS WHO CAN SPLURGE
Going Out

Brought to you by William

As you get older, there is less pressure on keeping the costs down. You have financial capabilities and can consider a wide variety of experiences and meeting places. When you want to go beyond a quick "coffee" meeting, try one of my favorite ideas.

❖ **Dinner at a cozy little restaurant** with good food and drinks. A quality ambience will allow you to focus on each other without distractions.

❖ **Scenic afternoon drive in your sports car**—along Pacific Coast Highway in California, for example. Enjoy the outdoors, do some sightseeing, and stop at a favorite hangout for lunch or dinner.

❖ **Concert.** A great way to have some crazy fun. Nothing like good live music and a crowd to raise your energy level. The key here is to pay extra and get the best seats possible.

❖ **Live professional sporting event.** Assuming you both like the same team and sport, this can be great fun and relaxing. It could be the Yankees, Lakers, 49ers, PGA and Tiger Woods, figure skating, whatever. Again, pay extra and get the best seats possible.

❖ **Comedy club show.** There's nothing better than a night spent laughing. It doesn't need to be a nationally known comic; just make sure the club meets your quality standards.

Regardless of your budget, there are some important things to avoid:

- ❖ **Playing tennis or a round of golf at your club.** This breeds too much competitive tension. Not good. One person is always better than the other and it makes the less talented person feel awkward.

- ❖ **Scary adventures.** Mountain climbing, skydiving, bungee jumping, and wildlife safaris, to name a few, are best left off the dating itinerary. *Adrenaline flow* to you might mean *fear* for your date. Not good.

If the signs ain't right, you must take flight.

Right about now you've reached the point where everything is going great. It's hot, steamy, and your special somebody is fantastic. She or he gets your adrenaline pumping, your temperature rising, and your ship capsizing. You're about to tell your homeboys and homegirls to prepare to meet the person you've been dating because things are so perfect. So, this means you're ready to cruise into the next exciting round of dating. By now, you are feeling more than a sexual vibe, you are feeling something deeper that can sustain a relationship.

However, it's still early, and there may be things you aren't seeing since the air is so steamy. It is at this point that you must look at a few bigger and deeper issues. We call these *Red Flags.*

Red Flags mean one thing: stop. To use a Johnnie Cochran-type statement, "If the signs ain't right, you must take flight." Caution Flags often require you to be more patient, be more introspective, or use different strategies. But Red Flags command you to pay attention, cut your losses, and leave. You simply do what Snoop Dogg says and "drop it like it's hot."

You're not playing around. The dynamics between you and whomever you're dating are coming to the point where you gotta be real and true to yourself in order to be a winner at the end of the dating game. Are you seeing some serious warning signs of jealousy or immature behavior? Do you get a strange feeling that you aren't truly getting to know the person you've been seeing for weeks or months? These may be indicators that something serious, unhealthy, or abusive may surface down the road. Often, the Red Flags pop up early. You can sense something is *not right* even before you finish your Top 5 List analysis on your new flame.

In this chapter, we'll discuss the Red Flags we believe are important to watch for in order to avoid a potentially negative situation. These are not listed in any particular order. We encourage you to think deeply about each and every one, particularly if you are dating someone who may have one or more of these characteristics.

Lauren's <u>New School</u> Red Flags

→**Mean to People/Strangers/Animals**

We've all been a little bitchy at some point or another. It happens every now and then. But, as a person who worked in the service industry, I can tell you that mean peeps are the ones who make a huge impression, and not the good kind.

When I was a server at an upscale restaurant, I had to interact and try my best to fulfill the needs of strangers, since that was exactly what my job entailed. Surprisingly, more than ninety-five percent of those I met were super friendly. When I did run into the rare few who insisted on being rude and demeaning, it was hurtful. No matter what I did, there was no pleasing them. And on top of that, they would complain to my manager. Now, don't get me wrong, I made some mistakes, but that didn't mean a complaint needed to go down. Each time that happened, I would say to my co-workers: "What kind of person would be rude just for the heck of it?"

> ***You can't change a mean person.***

When I go out on a date, I always watch how the individual treats the server, cocktail waitress, or bartender. Is she respectful? Is she bossy? I'm not saying she has to strike up a conversation and get the person's life story. That would be sort of inappropriate. However, saying "thank you" and smiling is a must. After being in the hospitality industry, I know firsthand how much work goes into serving and it's great to hear words of appreciation. So, when my date is nice and genuine to them, their score goes way up in my eyes. If they're good to strangers, they'll probably be good to you. If they're absolutely rude, then I'm thinking, *What's the fastest way outta here?*

→Secretive

We've all got thangs that we don't want to tell others. And, frankly, some information should be kept to yourself, like when you snuck into your parents' liquor cabinet and drank a little champagne while they were out or, that as a teenager, you used to sleep with everyone within a four-mile radius. These mistakes are part of life. However, when you're trying to get to know someone romantically and they seem to duck 'n dodge your questions, avoid going into their personal life, or refuse to give you details about what is considered basic information, then you gotta take a moment to stop.

One night I was hanging with my friends at a bar in West Hollywood and a woman approached me. She complimented my looks and asked for my phone number. A few days later we went out on a date and I ended up having a glass of wine at her place. We talked for an hour or so and I learned that she was a personal chef. Later, I noticed she didn't have a lot of food in her house. Plus, she didn't offer to cook anything. I've known chefs and they always had numerous products, food, and related items around their home. She had nothing. Still, I thought, *Lauren, don't assume. Just go with the flow.* One night, her good guy friend came over and whispered that they were married so he could come to this country legally. When I asked her about it, she refused to tell me when it was or any details about it. For all I knew, they could have been lovers. Flat out, I got bad vibes. On top of that, she said she was making a lot of money as a personal chef, but decided to move into a much smaller place to "save money so I can travel to China." If she made a lot of money as a personal chef and got a gift of a brand-new BMW from the man she married, then wouldn't she have moved into a bigger home? Yeah, it didn't make sense, which is why I stopped seeing her.

→Controlling/Jealous/Possessive

For me, these qualities are one and the same. If you're dating someone who keeps blowing up your phone, then he's not just jealous and possessive, but also really controlling. He wants to know where you are and who you're with. He's all about marking his territory and letting you know that he runs your town, not you. Whoa! And you thought Halloween was scary. He's his own haunted house. One that you don't want to enter. Ever.

Fortunately, these types are easy to pinpoint. Like a guy who always orders what you'll have to eat and drink when you go out together or a woman who makes you cut her steak (I've seen it). Another example

> - L -
> On a different note, an amusement park haunted house is a great first date since it forces you be physically close.

is someone who sends you a text each morning that says, "Where you at?" That's not trying to get to know you or simply say hello.

One time I went out with someone who was showing warning signs of being possessive. She would ask me who I was going out with or what I was doing over the weekend. This was after only two dates. When she found out that I had a date planned with someone else, she blew up. For me, this was a huge Red Flag that ended any romantic possibility. It's completely normal to date a few people at the same time, and she couldn't wrap her head around it. I am not cool with a volatile and controlling person, especially after just a few dates.

→Drinking Around the Clock

Don't get me wrong, I love a nice glass of wine or maybe even several mimosas after a long workweek. There's nothing better than coming home and getting on the couch with some merlot and potato chips. But you won't ever see me doing that before 5:00 p.m. or on a frequent basis. That would be starting a very bad and *not so sexy* habit.

I once dated a woman who loved to have a drink in the morning. I never thought anything of it until, on her birthday, she got terribly drunk before the sun went down. She was running around her apartment and repeatedly falling down on her face. I remember crouching down beside her and thinking to myself, *this girl has a problem.* It really broke my heart to watch. Even more shocking to me was the fact that I didn't see this unhealthy behavior earlier. It never occurred to me that her behavior was that of an alcoholic. I just assumed that it was what most young people did. But, in reality, it was destructive behavior that should have been addressed due to its serious nature. After I told her to get help, she refused and denied having a problem. That's when I knew the situation probably would not improve. Did I quit dating her because of it? Not the first time, but I did after we dated for a second time.

> - W -
> How much is too much? Drinking two to three glasses of wine every night or half a bottle of vodka is serious and that person may need to get some help.

Let's Break It Down
It's your choice

Lauren: If you're going to stop dating a man or woman for something, their alcoholism is an understandable reason. *Best-case scenario*: He stops drinking and then you're always the one having fun while he reluctantly sips on a virgin margarita. *Worst-case scenario*: He continues to be an alcoholic and you'll have to constantly deal with a hot mess. ***You are not powerful enough to make 'em stop wanting to get wasted. I never believed those words until I went through it with an alcoholic.*** Don't feel bad for choosing yourself and leaving.

→"V" Syndrome

Let me start out by saying that no one has a perfect relationship with their family members. We all struggle with family dynamics and that's completely normal. My dad and I grow closer all the time, but we're still working on our relationship. It will always continue to develop and improve. For others, a relationship may not be possible with certain family members due to abuse and disrespect, for example. This is a reality for millions of people, and a hard one to swallow.

There are a select few who refuse to talk to their family for petty and ridiculous reasons, like the fact that they won't take care of their financial responsibilities or that their family won't support their dreams when, let's say, it's a detriment to their health or not positive. I don't know any functional parents who would consider supporting their child if he chose to become a pot dealer. What it comes down to is that this type of person is determined to stay a *Victim.* Everyone else is at fault except them.

When you're faced with a guy or gal speaking about their family in a negative way when they seem loving and kind, ask more questions. If they're upset because of debt after traveling the world and can't deal with the family not coming to the rescue, then that's definitely a sign of immaturity and self-centeredness. You may even face a person who goes on and on about how their parents wouldn't accept their ex-partner. Dig deeper. Yeah, you may find out that they are racist, homophobic, or prejudiced in some way. But there's also a chance that the reason was that the ex-partner had a drug habit and was very abusive.

There is always another side to the story, which is why I always try my best to get as much information as I can before taking a strong action. The worst thing would be pushing someone away without knowing all the sides. But hey, once you do, be real with yourself. If homeboy or homegirl is trifling and you know it, don't waste your time.

→Emotionally Unavailable

We've all heard the phrase, "I want what I can't have." Most of us can relate to crushing on a cute guy or gal whom we had no chance at dating. They were completely out of our league or just not into us. I've had more than a few in my life who wanted nothing to do with me. Funny

> - **W** -
> Sometimes by trying too hard, you can come off as desperate. Take your time and relax so that things can come naturally.

enough, I thought I had a shot as long as I kept on trying to get their attention.

I have a gay friend named Mark who started going out with a doctor after he asked Mark out on a date. On their first date, he took Mark to a nice French restaurant, where they had wine and salad. Mark was completely impressed and flattered by the way he was treated and admired the doctor's soft, gentle nature. Later that night, Mark went to the doc's place, where they each drank a bottle of wine— white for the doc and red for Mark. Mark loved this, too. A few hours later, the doctor came out of the bathroom with a toothbrush and said, "You're definitely not the type to go to bed without brushing your teeth." Mark smiled at this and decided to stay the night, since the doctor insisted the streets of New York would be safer if Mark didn't drive home tipsy. Mark changed into some of the doc's clothes and they snuggled in bed, plus some light kissing.

As the weeks went by, Mark only heard from him once a week. It was always the same day and the same time. And he would always invite Mark to the exact same French restaurant, where they would have salad and wine. Then they would talk for a few hours at his place, drink a bottle of wine each, and snuggle. Nothing ever changed, and no matter what Mark did, the doctor would always keep Mark at an emotional distance. This went on for months until Mark was finally able to realize that the doc would never let him inside on an emotional level. Even to this day, Mark occasionally emails or texts this man in the hope that he'll change. He still hasn't.

Emotionally unavailable peeps, more often than not, are sexy and seductive. For whatever reason, whether it's from childhood issues or plain sexual chemistry, we can't say no to them and do crazy things that are out of our character in order to get their attention. Does it make sense? Not really. I'm sure if we paid a shrink $40,000, we could get to the bottom of it. But seriously, these types are extremely detrimental to our heart, soul, and spirit.

But many of you are still wondering, "How do I know when the person is unavailable?" Oh, *you know.* Intuition is our biggest asset. It's in the way the person talks to you or tells you only so much. Perhaps he's only available for dates once or twice a month. Maybe she never touches you or only occasionally gives you affection. Maybe you've never met his friends, family, or co-workers. If you notice that you're not learning about or getting to know that woman or man you've been seeing, then something ain't right. It may be time to either hit the brakes or insist on knowing more information. And if you don't get it, no second chances. Just nicely break it down that you aren't a good match and keep movin'.

→Bad Communicator

It's tough for any relationship to work when the communication isn't solid. In the beginning stages of dating, everything should be easy and breezy. This is the honeymoon. The relationship will never get simpler than this. So, in my eyes, basic things are critical, like being able to understand the other person without any issues.

For example, let's say you're the type who deals with conflict by sitting down and maturely discussing your point of view with the other person. You happen to be dating a wonderful woman who deals with conflict by shutting down and refusing to talk about her feelings or thoughts.

> - L -
> You should be sipping on margaritas on the beach right now. Not throwing them at each other in frustration.

When you give, she pulls away. This doesn't mean she's a bad person—this is just how she communicates. From my experience, these situations don't get better. You'll always be the one giving more while they back away and remain quiet. A good communicator and a bad communicator have little to no shot at a healthy, long-lasting relationship. Getting on the same page is as difficult as finding a fitness addict in a fast-food restaurant.

William's <u>Old School</u> Red Flags

Ugly Personality or Looks←

There are two kinds of ugly. First, is a *bad personality.* These people are self-centered, rude, negative, sarcastic, and critical about everything. Except for certain moments, like sexual encounters, they are hard to spend time with. The second kind of ugly is *physical appearance.* It's common to meet someone who doesn't look anything like her Internet photos or the way a

> - W -
> A woman might look like Halle Berry in a computer picture, but just the opposite in person. Whoa, that would definitely not be a nice surprise.

mutual friend described her. If it's a feature you cannot accept with ease, it should stop the show. In any case, you are not obligated to do therapy on a bad attitude or surgery to make someone attractive. Don't try to fix it. Ugly is something you can't fix. You are burning valuable time and energy, so consider ending things.

Beautiful can be ugly. There is nothing more unpleasant than an attractive person who has an attitude. When you go for the looks upfront, you are going to experience many of these people.

I remember when I dated Sheila, a really hot sista— tall, broad shoulders, small waist, knockout booty, and great legs. She looked good in everything she wore. In public, heads always turned for a second glimpse. No wonder she thought everything revolved around her. I really loved the eye candy, so I endured several evenings of dinner and dancing. After a night out clubbing, we arrived back at her place and I made my move. She let it happen, but it was not good. She was like a bag of cement. While lying there, I thought about the way she talked down to the waiter at the restaurant and had several dishes sent back to the chef. She never said thank you when I did my gentlemanly stuff and never complimented me about my new sports car. Everything was about her. She was never curious about me or the world in general. But she was quick to point out someone's poor attire, bad makeup, or how much they were overweight. Was that all she had to offer? Too bad, because I needed more to mentally engage me. No wonder I couldn't get into things in the bedroom. This girl was ugly, as in ugly attitude. I decided to get up and leave. I didn't need it that bad.

Boozers and Users←

Substance abuse comes in many packages. For the middle-aged crowd, alcoholism is the most common one. My radar goes up when I see my date have one drink too many on multiple occasions or if she's always sipping on something when we get together. I call them Boozers. I must admit, they can be fun dates, but once the juice starts flowing, it's off to crazy land. They let go of all their inhibitions, sometimes with you and sometimes with others. It usually results in something embarrassing going down. Boozers are masters of the morning-after apology calls. Let them go.

> - W -
> As an Old Schooler, these things matter even more as health issues pop up more frequently.

Number two on this list is smoking. Hate it. Who needs the bad breath, dangerous secondhand smoke exposure, and funky-smelling clothes? In my thirties, I met a cute flight attendant named Pamela. We dated several times before I found out she smoked. One evening we started fooling around and then the ultimate French kiss went down. *Oh no, cigarette breath.* It tasted like I had just stuck my tongue in an ashtray of cigarette butts. She wanted to continue; I wanted to find the Listerine bottle. Like a caring person, I tactfully told her about her breath, and she was embarrassed. Anyone can have bad breath, but the big picture is long-term health issues. Do I want to take my journey through life with a partner who smokes? That's a no.

Lastly, the most serious abuse is pharmaceuticals. It's understandable when someone is diabetic and using insulin, or using medication for other legitimate health issues. But I'm referring to a dependency on illegal drugs—coke, crystal meth, uppers, sleeping pills, and the like. These abusers are usually a mental and physical mess. They operate on the dark side—i.e., deceit, physical abuse, stealing, and other irrational behaviors. Their chemical dependency is their passion. Look out. They will hurt you to protect their habit.

All Talk, No Listen←

This isn't about using good English. Nope. I am referring to the inability to communicate effectively. First, all talking and no listening. This is a bad combo. Nothing drives a guy away quicker than a lady who runs her yapper all the time. No wonder she doesn't understand you and you two don't connect on a substantive level. With *talkers,* everything stays on a superficial level, and they assume a lot. Talkers don't usually invest enough time and energy listening, probing, and observing.

The second type of bad communicator is the *quiet, nonverbal type.* They have limited social skills and are boring to be around. With these dates, you never know where you stand. You are typically the last to know. Too much like cat and mouse. These people think you can read their minds. And when you miss a cue, it's like you did something wrong. That's just bullcrap that I don't have the patience for.

Third, there are the *miscommunicators.* Out of convenience or game playing, these types often don't share vital information. Call it "selective sharing." They operate in a way that protects their true feelings or something that they are hiding. Withholding information is not the same as lying, but it's very close. Games—who needs that?

Dishonest←

Tell me the truth and nothing but the truth. What's so hard about that? Scared to hurt someone's feelings? The truth cannot hurt more than deceit, cheating, and lying.

It's terrible to drift around in the clouds not knowing something and then feel totally betrayed when you discover the truth. A buddy of mine started dating a lady who I had sexual encounters with a long time before their involvement. She always avoided group get-togethers, using all types of excuses. After this had gone on for several months, he confronted her by asking, "What's the deal here?" She finally admitted what had happened between us, and my buddy was blown away. Her last comment was "I thought you knew." This could have been avoided had she been honest upfront. It felt like deception; it felt like she was hiding something much more important. My friend couldn't deal with that.

> **- W -**
> Should you tell your friend if you've slept with someone they are dating? It's up to you. I would say yes, but prepare for hurt

Ceci was the lead singer in a local band. My buddy Al started dating her. They both committed to a monogamous relationship. He would go to many of the band's local gigs and loved the response Ceci got from the crowds. The band often did overnight trips, but Al never went. After a few months of dating, Al discovered he had a VD. He confronted Ceci and she acted stunned and somewhat hurt. But one of the band members liked Al and told him confidentially that Ceci had an on-and-off dating relationship with the drummer. Al was surprised. He confronted her, but she would only admit to a one-night "mistake" with him that happened many months before she met Al. Weak story. Al's medical condition could only have come from Ceci. Why not admit to being unfaithful since the evidence was undeniable? That's definitely something that would make me open the door and say, "See ya."

> **- L -**
> This is a good reminder to always get tested periodically throughout the year.

Damaged Goods ←

When you've been out there for a while, like I was, you always run into someone who is recently out of a bad relationship. Often, they are still in need of some mental and emotional repair, but may not know it. Early in the conversation, you find out she has a child and that the baby's daddy is dangerous or he just ended a long-term relationship or marriage because his partner left him for someone else. Often, these people are using their new dating partners to escape their hurtful past. They think that getting back out on the scene as soon as possible will heal the wounds. I call these *Rebounders*.

Be careful. In these situations, the person is probably not finished with a past relationship. There is still anger, fear, or possibly love remaining for an ex. What you have here is a person who is incapable of committing to a new, healthy dating relationship. Your goals and timing won't match theirs. Their motives won't be the same as yours. Deep in their subconscious thoughts, they're comparing you to someone else, being paranoid, and not able to trust things and let go. You can't fix this big, raw wound right now.

It reminds me of Teresa. We flirted with each other for several years, but we were both in relationships and couldn't connect. She was a former model and had a great, outgoing personality. When I learned she had broken up with her high school sweetheart of eight years, I called and she quickly responded. To clear the decks, I created an issue with my

> - W -
> Sometimes, you can't force it to work no matter how hard you try.

lady so that we would break up (yeah, I was a bad boy) and Teresa and I could hook up. She was someone I dreamed about. Now, it was actually happening. After six months of steamy dating, I was hooked. She rocked my world. Then, one day, we had a disagreement over something silly. She left upset and we didn't talk to each other for a few days. Then, she came over and broke the news to me: She was getting back together with her ex. Three months later, they were married. I was in denial for a long time. But I had to accept that she never fell out of love with her ex, and I didn't have enough time or horsepower to pry her away.

And then, there was Darlene. Fly, oh my. Mutual friends wanted us to get together. I agreed to a double date with my buddy and her younger sister. We had a great time, although I noticed Darlene was a little quiet. On the next few dates, she came out of her shell and I got really excited about her. She was a beautiful girl, sophisticated style, very feminine, sexy, and easy to talk to. After several weeks, I was willing to focus on her, but she was obviously holding back. A few more dates and I pushed with my best charm. Still, she held back. Dang. Then, without notice, I got a phone call from her sister. She confessed that Darlene's ex was serving life in prison for murder. She had been in a long-term, abusive relationship and he was still messing with her mind. This was hard for me to comprehend. But, at that time, she was damaged goods and incapable of being in a healthy dating relationship. It was hard to let go. That would have been a dynamite hookup, but not worth the pain and frustration.

Still Married ←

Wait until the divorce is final.

So, you recently start dating someone and you're seriously thinking about a future together. Then, you discover he or she is "not yet" divorced. *Put on the brakes.* You are playing some dangerous odds if you keep betting on this horse. In the overwhelming majority of these situations, you don't get through their entanglements and personal issues. There is no happy ending where you ride into the blissful sunset. It's more of a feeling of being punked.

There are many reasons why these relationships don't work out. Here are just a few:

- Still emotionally tied to their "soon to be" ex
- Still financially tied to their "soon to be" ex

- Guarding themselves against a serious relationship
- Just looking for "support" to help them make the final break
- Using you to make their "soon to be" ex jealous

So, the divorce is not final yet? Okay. Ask these questions in this sequence:

1. When did you file?
2. Who filed?
3. In what county and state did you file?
4. Have you been to court yet?
5. Do you have a lawyer?
6. Where are you with a property settlement agreement?
7. Who is getting the kid(s)?
8. Are you still living in the same house?
9. When will it be final?

You might have a chance if they filed a year ago, have their own place, have a good job, and the divorce becomes final the next day. Otherwise, *run.*

Your Red Flags

By now, you probably have an idea of what you can and can't deal with in a relationship. This is always helpful, but putting these things down on paper will be a good reminder and bring you back into focus when you need it most.

Use the box below to write out a list of your most important Red Flags.

```
┌─────────────────────────────────────────────────┐
│                 My Red Flags                    │
│                                                 │
│    1)  _____  │
│                                                 │
│    2)  _____  │
│                                                 │
│    3)  _____  │
│                                                 │
│    4)  _____  │
│                                                 │
│    5)  _____  │
│                                                 │
└─────────────────────────────────────────────────┘
```

Chapter Summary

Keep in mind that no one is perfect. We're all going to have our own imperfections. Dating is all about seeing whether or not we can deal with those imperfections. In terms of your Red Flags, only you can decide what those truly are. We gave you our list, but yours may be different or include many more or less. There are no wrong or right answers. But if you don't stop at alcoholism, lying, emotional unavailability, or toxic behavior, then you have no one to blame but yourself.

William's Old School Wisdom	Lauren's New School Wisdom
When you discover a Red Flag condition, walk away immediately.	People who are set in their ways now will more than likely never change. Holding on to the hope that someone will be different for you is a huge risk.
Trying to date a person with Red Flags is distracting you from spending time with really exciting and fun people.	Date as many peeps as you'd like, as long as you communicate with each person you're seeing.
If your friends and relatives dislike the person you are dating, take note.	Pay attention to your intuition and listen when it's saying, *this ain't right.*

PEEPS ON A BUDGET
How to Shine Your Crib

Brought to you by Lauren

There's nothing better than being able to host a date night at your place. You not only save money by doing this, as opposed to going to a restaurant, but you also have the opportunity to impress. Therefore, your pad needs to be on point. This is the first thing that your new Boo sees once they step into your home. So, it's critical to make your space represent who you are to the best of your ability on a budget. Here are some tips.

❖ **Hit up IKEA for the small things:** decorations (paintings, sconces, creative lighting, and so forth), hip kitchen accessories, television stands, chairs, bar stools, and more. Buy a few $10 paintings and hang them on your living room wall. Put a $30 floor lamp underneath to make them pop.

❖ **Visit small neighborhood furniture stores.** Most people think these places are expensive, but many aren't. Also, their items tend to last longer and be sturdier than commercial spots. Look for reasonably priced couches, loveseats, leather chairs, dining room tables, and the like.

❖ **Check out thrift stores/Salvation Army.** These places will surprise you. Often, people donate nice items like beds and other kinds of furniture. My friend often shops at a thrift store in Beverly Hills and finds great things for her home.

❖ **Throw down some area rugs.** You can find good deals on large rugs at Target, Ross, and Kmart. I just bought a beautiful one for my living room for $75 at Kmart, which was marked down that day. Also, remember to check out special deals by looking online or in the newspaper.

❖ **Update your appliances.** You can throw out that television from 1998 since flat-screen televisions are so cheap these days. Also, check out places like Target and IKEA for microwaves, toasters, coffeemakers, and more.

❖ **Get some houseplants and scented candles.** Plants will keep air circulating in your home, plus make things look vibrant and fresh. Using candles and air freshener will give your place a sexy vibe while making it smell good.

❖ **Display personal items.** This can be a photo album that you keep on a coffee table or souvenirs from the places you've traveled. Best of all, while these things are often the cheapest to add to your crib, they are often the most meaningful.

In order to shine your pad and not bust your wallet, you have to search and be willing to hit up store after store to find the best deals. It's worth it.

PEEPS WHO CAN SPLURGE
How to Keep Your Pad on Point

Brought to you by William

Whether you've been out of the game a while or lost half your stuff to your ex, your crib deserves critical attention. Like good dental hygiene, your pad speaks volumes about you and what you are about.

- ❖ **Hire an interior decorator** to assess your pad. It will cost you a couple hundred bucks, but you will get some dynamite advice on home improvement ideas.

- ❖ **Home furnishings** need to have comfort, flow, and a hip/contemporary flair.

- ❖ **Always buy quality stuff and stick with your overall design plan.** Avoid picking up random items just because it's unique and the price is right.

- ❖ **Make your home about comfort and class.** For me, it's important for my crib to have large living room pieces, nice art throughout, a surround-sound system, a family room with at least a sixty-inch, flat-screen TV, comfortable lounging, and a bedroom that invites.

- ❖ **Have a well-appointed bar** with a good selection of red and white wines.

- ❖ **Pay some attention to the kitchen.** Keep it simple, but always have some good dishes and flatware for that special guest.

- ❖ **Get a housekeeper.** People on the go don't have time to be their own maid. It may be once a week or once a month. Keep sloppy out of your game.

5.
Slow Your Roll!

You ain't getting on that plane to Love Land if your ID is chilling at home.

Oh boy, right about now, you're on cloud nine. The person you've been dating is not a Quick Hit. What you have feels like the real deal. This is often called the *honeymoon phase,* which means you're probably a month or two into dating, maybe even more. Your special new person can do no wrong at this time and everything seems perfect. Even the trash you took outside smells like roses. You did your due diligence on the Caution and Red Flag sections, so all systems are still go. The feelings are right: Top 5 List is satisfied, he or she is very intoxicating company, and you can't keep your hands off each other. We get it—you waited a long time and screened this one the right way.

When you get to this stage, you have answered some key questions. This is more than just someone to date and have some fun with every once in a while. It's not a niche relationship, such as dinner dates, sexual benefits, or escort decoration. No, this is a possible keeper and potential long-term partner. And you are ready.

But before you go any further, it's time to *tap* on the brakes. Regardless of these great feelings you're experiencing, you must ask yourself:

Have I checked my speed? Are we going too fast?

There is no golden rule about how fast two people can fall in love. The important thing is how you handle your emotions when it happens. At this time, when you're almost falling, rational thinking gets lost in the fog of steamy romance. So, what we advise is simple: **Enjoy the bliss, but avoid hardcore commitments for six months.**

What are the hardcore commitments to *avoid* (as in, *never do*) during this time? Thought you'd never ask. Here they are, in no particular order:

The Nine Hard-Core Commitments
1. Marriage
2. Moving in together
3. Consolidating your resources
4. Losing contact with your relatives or close friends
5. Relocating to be closer to each other
6. Dropping out of school or quitting your job
7. Giving up a cherished passion or hobby
8. Monogamous commitment immediately after a failed relationship/divorce
9. Having a baby

These nine *never-dos* during the first six months are sometimes hard to accept. But if things don't work out with you and your new Boo, it shouldn't turn your world upside down. The last thing you need following a terminated relationship is starting your life over. Sure, your heart may take time to heal, but you don't need to worry about finding a new place, looking for a job, or salvaging your bank account.

> **- W -**
> It's always good to have a backup plan in all areas of your life.

Lauren: When I was dating a woman during college, she paid for my cell phone after we had been dating only a few short months. It was nice and I didn't mind at all since my funds were so low. I had no job and relied on student loans to pay for my day-to-day expenses. After we broke up, I suddenly had to find the money to pay for my expensive phone bill. Looking back, I probably should have focused more time on getting to know her rather than saving a few bucks.

Let's Break It Down
Identify their personality

William: ***Don't forget to identify the personality type you're dating.*** Playas want to go fast, make empty promises, don't have a conscience, and have lots of bad intentions. The Ladies' Man will romance you slow, steal your heart, and ultimately will not commit completely. The Good Guy is just that: He may be a bit predictable and lack a little style, but the going will be safer, which isn't a bad thing. Give this type of person a chance.

What If . . .

Since we feel it's so important that you *not* make any major commitments in the first six months, here's a list of *what if* examples that you may encounter and should avoid doing too soon in the dating relationship.

> - She just called you and wants her mother to move in with you.
> - His new job is across the country and he's willing to pay for all of your expenses to make the move with him.
> - You're getting older and have a strong urge to elope.
> - The two of you get along so well you're both looking into adopting a child together.
> - It takes you over an hour to get to her place, which is why you want to give your boss two weeks' notice and find any job you can to be closer to her.
> - Rent is hiking up again and you'd save a ton of money by moving in together.
> - Mom and Dad keep calling

- W -
If you're getting pressured to make a major decision, don't budge. The right person for you will wait until you're ready.

---

you to grab a bite to eat, but you don't have time to return their phone calls in between work and making love.

➢ He doesn't like the fact that your tennis instructor seems flirtatious, so you decide to stop going.

➢ You take a leave of absence from college to travel the world with your new lover for a year or two.

We're serious about this, folks. If any of these situations come up during the first six months, step back. As much as we don't want to tell you what to do, *don't do it.* Having the baby can wait and so can moving to another city. These are major decisions that make major changes in your life. Pause, breathe, and keep it mellow right now. Just get to know each other for the time being.

How Do You Watch Your Roll?

1. Check Out the Basics
Now that you have an idea of where you may have skipped a few stops along the way, it may be time to backtrack. Within the first few weeks and months of dating, there are things you gotta check out before getting serious. Some of them may sound superficial because, well, they are. But hey, it is what it is.

See the Crib and the Car.
Lauren: This is an essential step in the dating process and can't be overlooked, no matter how strong the connection. You may be dating a hoarder and not know it. Perhaps this person is still living with his mama who is paying the bills. Is his car well maintained? There's nothing worse than going into a dirty, smelly vehicle, particularly after you've fooled around with someone. It's sorta gross (unless it doesn't bother you).

> **- L -**
> There's nothing sexy about a smelly car full of old food, dirty shoes, and stale clothes.

As a young person I have to fight the urge to be disorganized and tell myself *I'll clean it up later.* I've seen the most disgusting dorms and apartments while in college, and also the cleanest. In most cases, you could never tell which person lived where by simply meeting them. Some of the most put-together peeps I lived with were very dirty. They would even talk about how messy their room or apartment looked. At the time, I never thought about how important it was for me to be around someone clean and neat . . . until I started dating a woman I'll call Fiona.

Fiona had a great job in the entertainment industry transcribing scripts into various languages for different companies. She dressed in professional attire every day, which was usually a business suit. When we started dating, I was impressed by her career and mental focus. So, as we went into her apartment, I never imagined feeling like I was in a bachelor pad. It was messy and uninviting. I felt uncomfortable and completely thrown off by the contradiction. But I was glad that I checked out her pad before I started to have strong feelings for her. Seeing all of that visual chaos turned me off real quick.

Where Do You Work?

Lauren: This has more to do with what they do with their time than anything else. You don't want to skip asking questions about this and then

> - L -
> Answers like "I just do stuff" or "Ya know, I work for the family" don't cut it. Ask for details and also, down the road, ask to check out where he or she works.

find out down the line that she's an exotic dancer or he's doing bookkeeping for one of the neighborhood gangs. By that point, you may be emotionally invested and not know what to do. If you ask these questions now and insist on getting details about what the person does for a living, you'll feel better in the end and know more about the person—which is what dating is all about.

You Have Kids?

William: A large percentage of single adults and middle-aged people have been in relationships or been married. Guess what? There is a good chance they may have had a child or two or three. Most secure adults are proud of being a parent and are up front about their parenthood. When they withhold some vital information, that's a real character flaw. If you are just dating and the cookie is good, you may not care about her little basketball team at home. But if *everything* is good, you *must* meet the kid(s) to see if you can be an acceptable part of the group. Do you see yourself always competing for their mom's/dad's time? Kids have the ability to slow your roll and even kill your chances of having a meaningful relationship.

Let's Check Your Blood Pressure.
William: In the twenty-first century, we find ourselves part of a global neighborhood. There's a variety of reasons for this—electronic technology, immigration, international travel, exchange groups, and so on. This gives us wonderful diversity of people, cultures, and knowledge. But in this more complex and diverse world, we are also more exposed to diseases, epidemics, and other health challenges. Often, heredity is the cause of certain health issues like heart disease and high cholesterol, but medical advances can allow people to remain viable when their quality of life would have been doomed twenty years ago. So, when you meet a wonderful person you want to date or have a relationship with, what you see on the surface may bring up some important health issue that needs to be discussed. Examples can be extreme obesity, addictions, hereditary diseases, lack of physical activity, and more. The person may decide to be forthcoming, and you may decide it's a non-issue and agree to continue. That's fine, because you are making an informed decision and nothing is being kept in the dark.

2. What's Yours Is Yours

Keep Your Keys.
William: This is something we all have a hard time doing when we're really feeling a guy or girl. But listen to me when I say this: Don't copy your keys yet. I suggest waiting until you're way past dating and into an actual relationship. I

never gave a woman the keys to my apartment unless I was serious about being with her.

Lauren: It sure feels good when someone you like gives you a key to their apartment. However, there's really no reason to do it at this stage unless you're house-sitting for a few days.

Once, a girl I had been dating for two months gave me a key to her apartment—because I asked her for it. This was way too fast and I truly didn't know her that well. But I was very focused on taking the next step and wanted the key for that reason. There was one occasion I was thinking of using it, but, to my surprise, she was very uncomfortable with the idea. I think if I had focused on slowing things down, I wouldn't have been surprised by her fear and reluctance.

I share this example to show that sometimes we think we're ready to make a big decision when we actually aren't. If you're thinking of giving your keys to someone, I would encourage you to think about why you're doing it and whether or not you're ready for this big step.

Don't Leave a Thang.

Lauren: I'm adamant about not leaving things at the house or apartment of the person I'm dating. My friends disagree with me on this, but they'll learn after losing a few precious items. This isn't to say you should be afraid to leave a sock or hair band, but be cautious. You can easily have a fight with someone you're seeing and never want to see him or her again. Well, say goodbye to those $150 high heels or that $200+ video game system you brought over during a boring night.

William: I may not be able to remember how many intimate encounters I've had in my life or the names of all the women I've dated, but I can tell you that I never left any important items at their house. And I always made sure they left with their belongings whenever they left my place. Why? It makes a statement, good or bad. When you leave something, it's like the beginning of marking your new territory. It doesn't matter what it is—toothbrush, underwear, spare clothes. Taking it with you is a subtle signal that you are keeping it noncommittal and neutral, and want to wait for the relationship to evolve.

Take your shiznit home with you.

Inhale, Exhale, Evaluate

Lauren: During the first few months of dating the exotic dancer I mentioned earlier, we always hung out during the day since we both worked at night. When we weren't hanging out, I would chill with friends or focus my attention on things she needed, like selling old furniture so she would have some extra cash (You'd think her profession was a consistently good money maker, but apparently the economy had a negative impact on the adult entertainment industry, too). The more we dated, the more I lost myself and the idea of what I was looking for in a partner. Friends would ask why I was seeing an exotic dancer and I would become angry. Instead of seeing that they cared, it seemed like they were judging her.

> **- L -**
> Being the one who does most of the work is never a good sign.

After a while, things changed when I was unemployed and had more time to myself. It was suddenly obvious to me that I was out of shape, so I joined a gym. I began to read more and do things for myself. I was also able to think about how I felt about her. Things had been going so fast that I hadn't allowed myself the time and attention to do this. Once I took time out to do so, it became obvious that we should see other people.

During the initial phase of dating, it's critical to be real with yourself. Sometimes, when we're in the honeymoon phase, we forget to do this. Like me, most of us have an eye on the prize, which can be that glorious six-month mark or simply getting to the point where you both verbally say, "We're official." Looking back, I was way too focused on the end result as opposed to living in reality, which was screaming, *You guys aren't right for each other!* Did she really hit my Top 5 List? Nope, but I was in it and blinded by her nice body and the distraction it was from the unhappiness I felt in my life.

> - **W** -
> Don't panic when you realize the person you've been seeing isn't right for you. Enjoy his or her company for what it is during the time(s) you share together.

William: While I was legally separated from my ex-wife, I met Ann, the hot flight attendant I mentioned in chapter 3. Based on mutual body language during the flight and the free wine she kept pouring me, I felt something intense happening. Lucky me. Ann's flight crew had a layover in the same town that night. We exchanged contact information and got together later. For several weeks, we would talk endlessly on the phone. At our next get-together, we could not resist the intense physical attraction. For the next few months, the scope and breadth of our intimacy had no boundaries. It dominated us. I paid little attention to details about her *soon to be* ex, her background, and her lifestyle. Then, on a trip back to Washington, I stayed at her place. I accidentally discovered her little black book. Too much information. I realized I didn't really know her.

I became more curious and asked more in-depth questions. She was uncomfortable talking about herself and some of her views were not compatible with mine. Turned out, we were mostly attracted on physical and sexual terms. This alone could not be the core of a long-term relationship. So, I changed my expectations and we continued to date for another four or five months. When my divorce was final, I decided to spread my wings and stay clear of relationships for a while. I was "damaged goods" and needed some down time to regroup. My dating relationship with Ann died as fast as it ramped up.

In the last chapter, I mentioned the problems with dating someone who is still married. So, what's the takeaway here? Ann came at the wrong time in my newfound single status. With Ann, I didn't take enough time to realize there wasn't enough for a relationship, and I was incapable of being in one with my marriage not distant enough in my past.

Unfortunately for Ann, she didn't see the signs. But it was hot while it lasted.

Chat With Yourself

Taking the time to consider whether or not things are going at a healthy and regular pace is completely normal—and necessary. We know this can be a hard thing to do, but don't worry. Here is a list of questions to consider answering:

> - Has it been hard to fit in anything outside of dating and work?
> - Did I establish a friendship before a sexual relationship?
> - In the past month, how often have I hung out with friends without my new Boo?
> - Have we had actual one-on-one dates or has it gone straight into relationship mode?
> - Does it feel forced in the bedroom?
> - Am I being persuaded to make a huge life-changing decision with this person?
> - Have I seen him or her at their best and worst?
> - Am I getting enough time for myself?
> - Am I feeling anxious?
> - Am I putting too much importance on this relationship?
> - Do I feel like I know him or her really well?

Have a private chat with yourself and ask some deep questions. Listen to your rational answers as well as your intuition. Be real. You may not know anything about your new lover since you've been going 120 miles per hour.

You're Dating, Not in a Relationship

We've all heard these words before at some point from a friend, sibling, parent, or maybe even a child. Sometimes, the lines between dating and a relationship can be blurry and confusing, particularly when we lead a busy life. And let's be real, many of us don't operate on both levels, because we tend to mostly be in relationship mode. You may be reading this and thinking, *Naw, that isn't me at all. I know the difference.* Others may be smiling, knowing that they go straight into wanting to act like a married couple without any awareness of boundaries or slowing things down a bit. No matter how old you are, man or woman, we all struggle with this at some point, but knowing the difference is essential to eventually finding success on the dating scene. It's critical to constantly remind yourself that this is the point at which the focus is on *getting to know who you're dating*—not on emotional intensity, fixing their problems, or whether you want to marry them.

Here are some examples of **Dating Protocol vs. Relationship Protocol** so that you can get an idea of the differences.

Your Boo is broke and needs money . . . your money?

Dating Protocol
William: Break it off ASAP. Don't give them a dime. Money problems say something about this person's character and lifestyle. Financial issues are the most common killer of marriages and close relationships.

> **- L -**
> It ain't hot when someone's money is always funny.

Lauren: Wish 'em luck and offer to research options for loans or financial assistance. If the person gets upset that you won't give your funds to their cause, then that's a huge Red Flag. If he or she is appreciative of your kindness and deals with it like a mature adult, that's a great sign.

Relationship Protocol
William: Protect yourself. One minor financial bailout might be acceptable. But, normally, people with money issues don't change. Let them go if this issue comes up again in the short term.
Lauren: Offer to write a check for the amount he or she needs—without expecting to ever see that *dinero* again. Now

you guys are in the struggle together while still having some boundaries. However, there has to be a limit.

He or she suffers from extreme depression.

Dating Protocol
William: Dating someone with this problem is not unusual. Generally, on dates, they are more positive and enjoyable. It's during their downtime (between dates) that the mood swings occur. If the dates are good, pick your opportunities carefully and go with the flow. You need to bounce when you see it going to the dark side.

> - L -
> Don't feel bad if you're not comfortable dealing with something like depression. Ultimately, your happiness matters most.

Lauren: I've been through this and it's tough. I think the thing to remember is that you have to do what's best for you, particularly as a young person. If you can't deal with it, that's okay. Dating someone who is bipolar, a cutter, and/or depressed requires patience and a level of understanding. At this stage, I would ask myself if I could deal with it or not. If the answer is no, then I would be honest about it.

Relationship Protocol
William: In a relationship, no way. That's too much time to experience the mood swings. Eventually, it can have a negative impact on you. It can drag you down and distract you from your own interests, job, and so forth. It's important to keep these people in a dating role and guard your heart. Limit your mental and emotional involvement.

Lauren: If both people are working hard to improve the depression, then that's all you can do. But if you're the only one trying to get things back on a healthy playing field, then that's a different story. Two people on a downward spiral won't help anyone.

Sex isn't happening as often as you'd like.

Dating Protocol

William: If you are not in a committed relationship, this shouldn't be an issue. You should have other dating options that fill the void. So, focus on the positives with this person.

Lauren: Since you don't know the person very well yet, you may be dealing with someone who has a low sex drive. If you think that's the case, then you can simply ask. Be real when you hear their response. I've been there and was honest about not being able to handle being intimate only a few times a month.

If the person you're seeing doesn't have a low sex drive, I think the same advice still applies. If you want it twice a day and the guy or gal wants that kind of affection twice a week, then hey, maybe you're both better off finding someone else who wants it at the same time.

Relationship Protocol

William: This is not something you can change easily. This should come naturally in a good relationship. If you discovered this as a problem in the dating phase, this is a Caution Flag or Red Flag. You can't have a complete relationship if this need is not satisfied. Address it early, fix it early, or don't go to the relationship level.

Lauren: You gotta pull out all of the tricks you know. Try to light some candles, put on a song by Maxwell, and get butt naked. Plan a long weekend away to one of the hottest spots in the world. Consider hiring a sex therapist.

Leave 'Em Wanting More

We all like a little mystery and surprise. The more we feel like there is to know, the more invested we become, whether it's a movie or a great book. If we went into the theater, sat down, and knew the ending in the first five minutes, most of us would leave, thinking there's no point in staying.

It's the same with dating. Taking it slow will allow you to see your new love interest layer by layer. You'll be able to appreciate and enjoy each moment to the fullest as you relax the pace and take time for yourself. Don't forget that it's okay to sleep by yourself on a frequent basis even though you're really feelin' the girl or guy you're seeing. Having this balance and connectivity to your home and space will be hard at first, but better in the long run.

Chapter Summary

It's never too late to switch up the game. After reading this chapter, you may be thinking you're way off course in terms of speed. Perhaps you can't even imagine only hanging out a few times a week or drastically slowing down the pace. Breathe it out and tell yourself, "I can do it." Then, do it one step at a time. If that person is right for you, they'll understand and respect your new boundaries and pace. Plus, think of how much stronger the sexual chemistry will be with more time between seeing each other. Hot, hot, hot!

William's Old School Wisdom	Lauren's New School Wisdom
Fellas don't have as much at risk going fast. Ladies beware—watch out for the Playas and their games.	Remember your priorities. Don't throw them out the window once Sexalicious enters the picture.
If the physical hookup happens early, you probably have a good dating partner, not a Soul Mate.	Spend at least thirty minutes a week *checking in* with the pace of your dating relationship(s).
If you are constantly being pushed to do something out of your comfort zone, ask yourself some tough questions about this person and the relationship.	For all the twenty-somethings and recent college grads: See your Boo two to three times a week at the most. Gotta keep that focus on!
After three months of dating, if you can't have fun doing nothing, you probably have a nothing relationship.	Be extremely verbal about your boundaries, not just with your date, but also with yourself.
The old saying "Fast-runnin' horses don't run long" is	If you communicate your need to go slower or faster,

| true in dating. Do everything possible to take it slow, particularly if he or she is a keeper. | stick to what you said. There's nothing more confusing than a person who has no idea what they want. |

6.
The Six-Month
Mark

Every driver has a blind spot.

You've reached a big chapter. You and your new romantic companion have made it to the six-month stage and things are going smoother than smooth. You can't think about anything else except how good you feel and your plans for the future. The road ahead is nothing but bright in your eyes, which is what you've been working so hard to attract.

On the flip side, however, maybe things aren't that ideal or consistently smooth between the two of you. Maybe you're torn because some days you feel like your Boo is The One, and then some days—bam!—the opposite feeling comes over you and the future suddenly looks doubtful. This is when confusion pokes its head into what used to be your cozy home and you're left wondering which way to go, or if you want to leave at all.

In this chapter, we're going to address these two possibilities and more. What do you do when you've started questioning whether that special feeling is real or just hoped for? It may take you out of your comfort zone as you reflect, but having clarity will give you the peace of mind you deserve. Life's short and we don't want you wasting any precious moments on someone who isn't on the same page; just as we want you to cherish that man or woman if that person is right there with you.

At six months, it's about *communication on all levels.* Check in with your love interest to make sure you're on the right track, even if it's going amazingly well. Also, seek out the wisdom of your close friends and family. Remember, most of us tend to be out of touch with reality when we're busy living on cloud nine and smelling the roses. Getting feedback from all sides can help tremendously. Make the effort and see what happens.

It's also very important to keep in mind that you're not committed yet. This stage is about *figuring out if you want to get a little more serious,* such as dating exclusively and having a drawer just for you at your new lover's crib. It's no longer the regular season, but you aren't in the Finals quite yet. However, if you continue playing with an excellent strategy and smart mindset, you will be.

Should We Keep Dating?

This is probably the first question to ask yourself at the six-month mark. If it's a quick, straight-up "No," then you've just saved yourself a lot of time and should now consider focusing on an exit strategy. If the answer is "Yes," it's time to delve deeper and get real by asking specific questions.

Get that pen and paper out. That's right. If you don't write your responses down, then you may forget (which some of us—*cough, cough*—have a tendency to do subconsciously). Fight that urge and press on anyway. Only by getting real and forcing yourself to express—on paper—how you're feeling will you be able to see if you have a good thang going or not.

Questions to ask yourself:

- Are we growing closer or further apart?
- How do I feel when I see him or her?
- Can I envision a long-term relationship with this person?
- Do we have great communication?
- Have we established a strong friendship?
- Am I satisfied with our sexual activity?
- Do we have curiosity, passion, and support?
- Are we competitive with each other?
- Do I trust him or her or feel slightly withdrawn and distrusting?

- Is it a struggle to find things to talk about?
- How often do we fight?
- Are there any signs of physical, emotional, or mental abuse?
- What was he or she like at their absolute worst?

By now, you hopefully have your answers—on paper—to these tough questions. Now what? It's all about taking your answers into deep consideration and figuring out how much they mean to you personally.

For example, some people don't care about good communication. Perhaps you prefer not talking about your emotions and feelings all the time. Maybe it's more important that you both support each other on a consistent basis.

> - W -
> But hey, let's be real, good communication is important in any relationship.

We're not saying your relationship must have certain traits or characteristics in order to last. Whatever *you* want is what matters here. The main goal is figuring out what that is and remaining true to your needs.

Be Open to Advice

Reaching out to a trusted and respected friend or family member about their opinion of your current relationship and partner is a good idea to consider, even if it doesn't impact anything. They can offer an objective and loving voice that often gets ignored when we're falling in love. This can be a hard thing to do at first, but once you get into the habit, it'll become second nature. In fact, you'll probably begin to make it part of your dating protocol. Keep in mind that just because you're asking for advice and feedback from someone doesn't mean there's something wrong. You're simply collecting information, just like you would for a survey.

Initiating that first conversation can be difficult. Whether you want to do it over the phone or in person, consider saying something to the effect of: "Hey, as you know, I've been dating this amazing guy (or girl) for a few months now and it's going well. Things are getting pretty serious and I'd love to hear any advice you have." If your friend is confused and wants to know what specific information you're asking for, then break it down: "Be completely honest with me. What do you think of the two of us together? What's your opinion of him (or her)?"

Do this with at least five to eight people and take notes so you can see if there are any consistent comments or concerns.

After doing this, or even before, some of you may be thinking, "Who cares what others think? I choose my partner, no one else." Okay. We understand that you gotta do what you gotta do, but know that you might be missing out on useful information from those who care about you. And hey, what do you really have to lose by asking? And is it fear of what you may hear that's stopping you? Is it the fear of going with what your heart says? Be real with yourself.

Let's Break It Down
Screw pride

Lauren: Many of us young people don't care what others think about the person we're dating, especially family. ***And for those of you who think you do, just wait until you find someone who makes you feel crazy and out of control. It definitely won't matter what mommy or daddy thinks when you're in love.*** I never used to ask my parents or friends what they thought about each person I was dating, but now I do. Why? Because I realized they have my best interests in mind, offer great wisdom, and give decent advice.

The Exceptions

Before you reach out to others for advice, keep in mind that there are *exceptions.* You don't want to ask just anybody. Uncle Ricci with four teeth and a big mouth probably can't offer you solid words of wisdom. You may also want to pass on asking your homegirl who thinks conflict is better dealt with by using fists as opposed to calm words. Here are some types to avoid confiding in.

1) Toxic friends and haterz

William: Years ago, I had a few friends who were against interracial dating. On one occasion, I met this beautiful Asian lady and we dated for several weeks before I felt it was time for her to meet my friends. When my two buddies became aware of her racial background, they immediately went into this negative bag—you know, all the reasons it wasn't right for me. I tried to force the issue by taking her to parties and group events with my so-called friends, but the tension was overwhelming. They just couldn't accept her, and she could feel this from them and see it in their body language. So, she decided to end our brief relationship because she felt the negative energy was too much too handle.

Frankly, I understand where she's coming from as I've reflected about it these past years. There's no excuse to dislike a human being for their ethnicity or the color of their skin. My mistake was not distancing myself from friends who discriminate, because they did not represent my values. For me, it was a lesson learned and a fine opportunity lost.

If you're dating someone who is of another race, or different than you in some way, and you know your friends won't support you, take a moment to ask yourself this question: *Are these the kind of friends I want to represent me around my new Boo?* That's what they are—a living, walking extension of you. I can't tell you who to associate with, but be mindful of the fact that you may be pushing someone amazing away because you're hanging out with people who don't represent your views.

Judging someone for who they are isn't cool, particularly as you get older.

Lauren: A hater can be a family member, best friend, or co-worker. The worst thing is going to a friend who has a big mouth or mean mentality and asking for love advice. They will more than likely steer you in the wrong direction, have a biased opinion, and not be looking out for your best interest.

We all have haterz or that token, crazy friend in our lives. What do most of us do with them? Laugh, have fun, enjoy their company—and keep them at arm's length. It's probably best to skip asking your friend who just got out of jail for stalking what he thinks of your new lover. However, if he mentions that they shared the same cell, that's something to look at.

2) *Auntie Jealous*

William: They come in all sizes and faces. In my case, it was my cousin. She had a close friend that she thought would be a perfect match for me. Instead of responding by asking the woman out, I ignored my cousin's attempts to get us together. At that juncture in my life, I was too busy being a Ladies' Man. Every time I saw my cousin, she would pull me aside and tell me all the things that were wrong with my date. Then it became clear that my dating exploits were distracting me from family time, and my cousin was probably jealous. I eventually realized that my cousin was emotionally fascinated by the possibility of her best friend hooking up with me. So, no one else in my dating portfolio got a fair chance from her. That's when I had to say to her, "Don't hate the playa, hate the game." Not surprisingly, she didn't like my cocky sense of humor.

Lauren: I hate to admit it, but I have plenty of these (not all aunts). No matter how amazing your lover is, they don't approve. You could say the person you're seeing treats you with respect and kindness, and your aunt or uncle would come up with some belittling or rude response. "Well, just because he treats you right, it doesn't mean anything if he doesn't make a lot of money." "So what if she's nice? It doesn't guarantee a future unless you guys are married." Somehow, they make you feel like the scum of the Earth *and* just plain stupid.

When I first came out to my mom about being a lesbian, she would often tell me that I wouldn't get far in the world because of my sexuality (among other things, like being overweight). It didn't matter that I was dating a great girl or that I was happy. She couldn't stop being rude and telling me about how it was a choice that I liked being with women. Now, I don't even discuss my love interests with her because I know she's not supportive.

3) Co-workers

William: This depends on the person. If you have a close relationship with one or two co-workers, getting their input on a dating relationship can be a good thing. Remember, they have no emotional or family biases. It can be good, neutral advice that you can take or leave. But no matter who it is, you must keep it from getting too graphic or too deep. The big negative is the possibility of people at work knowing your business; this is never a good thing.

Lauren: No one at work needs to know your business, especially if it's romantic. It doesn't matter if you've known that person for years and trust him or her with your life. Keep quiet about deeply intimate and private matters regarding your love life. It's cool to go into some things, but nothing that you wouldn't want a stranger to know.

Talking With Your Boo

First thing to keep in mind: *Discussing your relationship and where you see it going doesn't have to be a big deal.* This applies to people of any age. It's always good to do routine check-ins with your lover, perhaps every few months. Once a week probably isn't the best idea. There is definitely such a thing as over-communicating, which you want to avoid.

So, how do you start this conversation, especially if you're not used to communicating in this way or you feel like it will cause tension? We would first like to reiterate that *talking about your relationship doesn't mean something is wrong.* Think of this as a friendly conversation about the weather, if that'll help take the pressure away.

Lauren: I think older people have an easier time with this conversation. Actually, I don't know of anyone my age who has ever sat down and insisted on *checking in* with their honey or fella. It's sorta like "If it works, it works." And if it doesn't, then a breakup happens. There's really no in-between with us young peeps. "Compromise" is not really in our vocabulary.

> - L -
> Relationships don't work without a little compromise. So, please put the toilet seat down, fellas. And ladies, consider not saying anything the few times it's left up.

Does that mean we're not capable of doing it? Heck no. It's just hard, and why spend so much time on that when you can be making out or having fun—or when there are so many other options? To this day, I struggle with initiating this discussion, but I always feel better in the end. And, more often than not, so does the other person.

When the exotic dancer and I chose to go our separate ways the second time we dated, it was after we both came to the mutual realization and understanding that we were not growing closer after dating for several months. It wasn't a dramatic and mean conversation, although we were both hurt and disappointed. Sure, it took a while to actually stop fooling around, but hey, we eventually made it to that point.

William: Mature people have less of a problem being open and honest. We have been around the block a few times and know the benefits of not wasting time. Having frank discussions about the status of your relationship with another person is a healthy thing. It clears the air. Remember, time is valuable; you don't want to waste it on a bad relationship at any age.

The Approach

This is our recommended approach to start off the check-in conversation at the six-month mark. Feel free to adjust and add where you'd like.

Step 1: Let your Boo know that you'd like to talk. Make sure to do this on the phone or in person and not in a text. Also, keep in mind that it's probably a good idea to maintain a calm and collected voice. The last thing you want to do is make him or her feel like something is wrong. If they want to know exactly what you'd like to talk about, be honest and say, "Nothing's wrong. I just want to make sure we're both on the same page about our future since things seem to be getting more serious. Are you okay with that?"

Step 2: Ask when they can meet in the near future. Make a date and time, and confirm the exact location so there's no confusion. Also, don't leave it for a month down the line.

Step 3: Meet up with your lover and talk for at least twenty minutes. It may be helpful to take a look at your answers to the questions from the beginning of this chapter before your talk. Also, consider going back to all of the conversations you've had with loving friends and family. What did they say that was consistent? Even if you disagree with some of these points, put some focus on them since they kept coming up.

Step 4: Create an action plan. If you're on the same page and you hear everything that you want, awesome. You're on the right track. If it's apparent that the dating relationship isn't working out, although one of you may want it to be, make sure to communicate this before the conversation ends. "It sounds like maybe we should consider ending things." "I'm not as happy as I used to be and think it's best if we stop seeing each other." Once that comes out of your mouth or the other person's, stick to it. Going back and forth between two decisions only adds chaos and confusion, which is unfair to both of you.

How to Cut the Ties

For many of us, it's easier said than done to stop seeing the guy or gal we've been hanging with for so many months, particularly if they are sexalicious. You know who you are. Some of you may be in denial. You may have the best intentions to keep your distance, but will you have the strength to not pick up the phone when he or she calls? If you get a surprise visit involving a robe and little to no clothes underneath, will you be able to resist?

> - L -
> There's nothing worse than being known as the couple that always makes up and breaks up.

Life's tough enough without these temptations. Here are some ideas and strategies that we've used in the past to avoid putting ourselves in a tough situation with an ex-fling.

- *Don't go to the same places.* This doesn't mean stop going to the grocery store. We're talking about parks, movie theaters, and any other location you would frequent with the person you were seeing. If you used to go to a nearby ice cream shop every night, then you'd probably want to take a break from going there for the time being. Grab that flavor at the nearest grocery store and chill at home with friends as another option.

- *Avoid gossip and drama.* Inevitably, you'll run into people who don't know anything about your recent breakup. Skip telling mutual acquaintances your business and avoid going into details about what happened. "Oh, it didn't work out between the two of us." That's all you need to say, and if you go into specifics, prepare for the worst. Everything you say might go back to the person you were seeing and cause drama. Also, avoid badmouthing your ex-Boo. It may feel awesome at that moment, but it only makes you look and feel bad in the end.

- *No calling or texting.* Don't even go there. It doesn't matter if you're stranded and can't get a hold of anyone. Start walking and find a gas station or wait until a friend picks up the phone. Also, delete your unlimited texting plan if necessary. When you start having to pay 10 cents per message, you'll begin to rethink sending texts when you're drunk. You know how you are and what you need to do in this regard. Take precautions.

- *Return items within a week.* This may not be possible if things ended badly. You may be better off just leaving the stuff behind. But if there's no drama or bad blood, then make sure to do the swap of items within a week. The more time there is to reflect and miss each other, the higher the risk of going back to the way things were.

- *No physical interactions at all.* There are no exceptions to this rule. Don't ever touch your ex-dating fling again after deciding to end the relationship. This will only complicate matters and prolong the drama.

- *Put the pictures away.* We're not saying throw them away or that you need to run from the past. However, consider taking things that remind you of your ex-Boo out of your daily routine, so as not to stir up strong emotions on a frequent basis. It may impact your work performance and other relationships if you're always thinking back to how things used to be. Take the pictures and other items out of sight for a few months and give yourself a chance to heal.

- *Don't be friends too fast.* A friendship may not even be a good idea at all, but for some it actually works out better than when they were romantically involved. However, right after you two decide to stop dating, being friends shouldn't be an option for at least six months, if not longer.

Follow Your Intuition

Although we're giving you dating advice and have the best intentions for you, we also understand that sometimes you have to follow your gut. You can't go wrong if you listen to your heart and that wise voice in your head. Sure, there may be a chance you'll get hurt, but at least you went with your gut. The key is being safe and not compromising your needs and well-being while following your intuition. We know, easier said than done.

If you're still stuck about whether or not you should be dating the person you've been seeing, that's okay. Live with it for a while, even if it's a few weeks or months. Don't make yourself push someone out of your life and end up having regrets years or decades down the line wondering, *What would have happened if I had stayed with him or her instead of ending the relationship?* Reflect and enjoy each moment until you come to a conclusion.

There Are Plenty of Fish in the Sea

After reading this chapter, you've hopefully realized that you're either happy with the person you've been dating or that you aren't that satisfied. Perhaps you've even mustered up the courage to speak with him or her and revealed your thoughts and feelings.

No matter what the outcome of the conversation turns out to be, give yourself props for taking that huge step. If it's exactly what you want to hear, great. Continue communicating with each other and being very open about how things are going.

And to those who may have heard just the opposite of what they wanted, stay strong. We know how hard it can be, and we want you to keep in mind that the search for love may be long, but what's important is that you never give up.

<u>Chapter Summary</u>

It's important not to let strong feelings and emotions blur your vision and judgment. Make sure to check in with yourself and ask key questions, such as the ones in this chapter. The answers may surprise you.

Try not to let others dictate your actions, but remain open to feedback. The world won't come to an end if no one likes your new Boo, though it isn't a good sign. The key is listening to those who care about you and don't mind keeping it real, despite how you may react.

Remember, that all you have control over is yourself. Dating is about figuring out who you're compatible with and who you're not. There's no need to waste time if you know in your heart that things aren't working out. Eventually, you'll find The One and have no doubt about the future.

William's Old School Wisdom	Lauren's New School Wisdom
Things ought to feel natural and warm after six months. If not, check yourself.	Don't force it if things aren't working. You both deserve better.
Keep a tally on drama and games. If you have experienced this at six months, you are dating a ticking bomb.	Take a break from Facebook, MySpace, Twitter, and other social media sites after ending it with your Boo.
Is there equality in the relationship? One should not dominate the other in matters of importance and sharing in general.	If things have just ended, it's probably a good idea not to go out and meet someone new right away. We all need time to heal and reflect.
Just because the sparks are still flying after six months, listen to your gut if something is bothering you.	Even if things are going very well, continue making efforts to keep your dating relationship fresh.
When a friend or family member is negative about	It's okay if you don't see yourself marrying the

your dating relationship, check whether they have a hidden agenda or prejudiced views.	person you've been dating. People grow all the time and that may change. Be patient.

PEEPS ON A BUDGET
Gift Ideas

Brought to you by Lauren

Dating isn't cheap. Just going out to a movie once a week with your special somebody can be an extra $100 a month. Yeah, that's scary. So, for many of us, we don't have much left over after bills. Over the past couple of years, I've learned how to get creative. Here are some of my ideas that are perfect for a nice, sweet surprise.

- ❖ **House gift.** Pick up on what your special somebody needs in his or her place—some wine glasses, a small desk lamp, slippers, and so forth. You can't go wrong with what you buy since it's so thoughtful.

- ❖ **Personalized CD.** Put some of your favorite songs together and burn them onto a blank CD. This is always a winner because it shows that you're sensitive and willing to put a lot of time and effort into something.

- ❖ **Bamboo plant.** Hit up IKEA or a flower shop for this. These plants last forever and cost under $10. Not to mention they're cute and perfect for any kitchen corner.

- ❖ **Poem.** This will never go out of style. Who wouldn't love a poem written about them? But don't get your cousin Mikey to write it for you.

- ❖ **Incense.** It smells great, costs around $3 per box, and sets the mood just right. You may want to buy an incense holder for a few bucks just to make sure nothing burns.

❖ **Regular season tickets.** You should be able to get tickets to a baseball or basketball game for a reasonable price during the regular season. You may be in the last row, but it's something.

❖ **TV show taping.** You'll have a great time and see someone famous—for free.

❖ **Haircut/manicure.** Treat your new guy to a haircut. It shouldn't be more than $20 if you aren't doing anything special. And most women love getting their nails done. A nice manicure is less than $20.

❖ **Bottle of wine.** Find out if he or she prefers red or white. Then hit up a local wine store and grab a bottle for $15 or less.

PEEPS WHO CAN SPLURGE
Gift Ideas

Brought to you by William

An important accent to dating is giving and making her feel special. The little stuff carries a price tag, but will deliver huge benefits! It also sends a message about your feelings and style. These gestures are not everyday events, and remember to choose your timing wisely. Gifts are a great way to knock them off their feet.

❖ **Roses delivered to her doorstep.** A no-brainer and very traditional. This one always helps the cause.

❖ **Day at the spa.** There's nothing more comforting than a day of self-indulgence for the body.

❖ **Go shopping together.** For instance, kick it at the Beverly Center in Beverly Hills. You never know what might catch her eye, but insist on getting it for her—perfume, a great pair of pumps, handbag, and the like.

❖ **Meaningful personal items.** A basketload of great CDs, DVDs, books, and other collectibles that she has expressed as things she always wanted but never got.

❖ **Jewelry.** Expensive, but always a homerun. I prefer a simple necklace or bracelet with a few diamonds.

NOTE: Romantic trips are great, but I don't call them "gifts" because both parties benefit. However, there is nothing more fantastic than a getaway to an exotic place such as Mexico, Maui, or Hawaii.

7.
The Stand-
In

Just because you're on hold doesn't mean you can't be busy doing something else.

"No stress, no commitment."
"It's easy and something I'm used to."
"Just something to do."
"I'm in a tough place right now."
"I'm so bored, I need a little excitement."
"It's there when I need it."
"Something is better than nothing."
"Not my ultimate match."
"It's comfortable."

Sound familiar? If your current dating status can be described by one of these phrases, you may be in what we call the *funky zone.* This is when great love isn't coming your way, so you decide to settle for what works in the moment, even though you know it's not going to satisfy your desire to find a long-lasting partner. In other words, you're choosing to hang with what we call a *Stand-In* (or *Filler*) who acts as the C-star in the movie called *Your Love Life.* Keep in mind that these are not Quick Hits. Nope, these are people you hang out with on a consistent basis. Though it's probably best for some of you to end things, get out, and clear your head, others stay simply because it's fun and what you prefer.

For most of the book, our focus has been on those of you who want to seriously date and how to take your game to the next level. But we gotta keep in mind that there's a large group of people in the *funky zone* out there as well. No, these types are not cold-blooded; it may be due to other priorities or the temporary inability to find that special someone. Many people think they're ready, but aren't being honest about their willingness, or lack thereof, to do what's necessary to be in a relationship: genuinely commit your love to someone. Or maybe you haven't met the right person yet. Heck, some of you simply don't want anything to do with a relationship because, in your opinion, it's too much to deal with. Whatever the reasons may be, remember that by having a Stand-In, you run the risk of subconsciously blocking your true love from coming into your life.

William: It's all about visibility when you're single and looking. You have to *stick and move.* "Sticking and moving" is a boxing term. It means you are throwing a punch and being nimble. In dating, it's the ability to be on offense (going after someone you are attracted to) and not getting sidetracked from your objectives after rejection or a bad encounter.

As you wait for your ultimate love match, the most important thing is keeping yourself out there, maintaining a socially active lifestyle, and not being a prisoner to your cave. This means dating people. When you can't find the *perfect* person to date or have a relationship with, keep yourself out there, and don't feel rejected or think you're a loser. Don't go with the easy option of a Filler. Fillers take up too much time and inevitably take you out of the dating game when you should be *sticking and moving* so you can find The One. Now is not the time to settle. So, make it a goal to develop a circle of individuals to date who keep you positive and enjoying life in general. Otherwise, you may find yourself in a complicated and drama-filled situation—like behaving with a Stand-In as if you're in a real relationship. Always maintain proper boundaries.

Let's Break It Down
It's okay

Lauren: My dad and I have slightly different viewpoints about having a Stand-In in your life. *You are not a bad person for wanting to have a man or woman in your life who comes and goes—or someone with whom there's no deep romantic connection.* It's okay to just have sex, eat all day with a jobless fool, have fun without thinking, or do whatever you want if it's fulfilling your current romantic needs. *Don't let anyone judge or look at you as if you've robbed a pregnant woman.* Do what makes you *happy*. When The One comes, you can and will kick your Stand-In to the curb if you're willing and ready.

Having a Relationship With a Stand-In (aka Filler)

Lauren's <u>Pros</u>

- There are no strings attached. Forget feeling like you have to constantly check in with a daily phone call or be forced into having an emotional discussion about how your sex life is going. It doesn't matter since you two aren't striving for a serious, long-term relationship.
- Your guard tends to be down. When you aren't trying to impress someone all the time, you relax. Suddenly, you don't feel pressured to do or say the right things. A fart or two comes out and you don't even say, "Excuse me." For some, this allows them to feel free to be themselves. Nothing wrong with that.
- You can have your cake and eat the whole dang thang. So you're having a bad day and don't feel like talking. Cool. With a Filler, you don't have to explain anything. At least, that's how it should be since there are no obligations in the emotional arena.

- There are no expectations. You may see each other for a week straight or five times a year. Who knows and who cares? The two of you aren't on the same page because there's no need or desire to be reading the same book.
- It's fun. And if it isn't, then you should consider letting the Stand-In go and replacing him or her with someone who knows how to have a good time and relax. You have enough stress and worry with work, family, and the sudden surprises that life brings. Your C-Star has no right adding any additional worry to that list.
- It's perfect for someone in their twenties. I am a firm believer in exploring and making many mistakes, which is what being in your twenties is all about. We're all already a mess as we try to find out who we are and what our career is going to truly be. So, romantically, why not make mistakes now, be a little bad, and have fun doing it? No one wants to have regrets when they're fifty-something with a ring on their finger and thinking, *I wish I had been with more people.* Having a Stand-In allows the opportunity to truly cherish and know that what we have, when we've found it, is truly special and amazing. Sure, some of you can feel that way without having to date casually, but others, like me, aren't so lucky.

William's <u>Cons</u>

- Yeah, so there may be no strings attached with a Stand-In, but it really means that both parties are always looking for something better. Why don't I feel good about that type of relationship? Well, I don't know about you, but I don't like being second best or taken for granted.
- The convenience is nice, but who's zooming who?
- Someone in these arrangements usually gets hurt. Eventually, one person starts dating or getting

emotionally attached to someone else. Then, it gets complicated and stressful, feelings get hurt, and it becomes easy for tension to escalate. And I can tell you—fighting isn't my thing. Avoiding unnecessary plate throwing or yelling is best in this situation. Ditch the Filler immediately and focus on the new person in your life. If you don't, then be real with yourself and own up to the fact that you just aren't ready for a serious romantic relationship. Maybe even join a therapy group to delve deeper into why you feel this way.

- Stand-Ins can easily slip into the *regular* category because it's too easy. This means that you treat him or her like a new dating candidate by always going out and spending a lot of time together. When this happens, this person also becomes a *blocker* (the worst thing in the world for a single person trying to find the perfect someone). This can only be avoided if you stick to the appropriate behavior and way of treating a Filler, number one being: *Don't spend too much time together.*

  > - W -
  > Fellas and ladies, therapy isn't a bad thing. It doesn't mean something's wrong with you. Look at it as an opportunity for growth.

- Stand-Ins don't challenge or inspire you. You don't feel like being a better person or excelling at work. There's no need since mediocrity is enough with your Stand-In. Personally, I can't roll in this direction. I need my partner to inspire me to be the best I can be, to stay sharp, and to max out the happiness in my life.

Yeah, Lauren and I have different opinions about Stand-Ins. Some of this is due to our age difference. As you get older, it's typical to dislike wasting time and coasting along in dating relationships. If you are actively dating and playing the field, recognize who you are regularly hooking up with and in what category he or she belongs. The more honest you are with yourself, the more time you save. A Filler can waste a lot of your time if you allow that to happen.

The following is a list of our most common Stand-In categories. Some of these you've seen throughout each chapter; now, we're going to discuss more about what each type represents and means to us.

The Cast of Stand-Ins

William's List

1. *Niche Player*

These types come in different shapes and sizes, and can also be Fillers. All in all, folks, it's very difficult to find the total package. Until you do, you have to take care of yourself, have fun, and satisfy your needs. In my *old school* world, we dated people to match the situation—e.g., music lover, conversation piece, sex buddy, arm candy, or workout partner. It's important to keep in mind that a Niche Player doesn't always equal a cakewalk. They can have issues and may be time-demanding. If you allow yourself too many of these types of dating matchups, they will definitely block you from meeting your total package.

Imagine having a Niche Player in your life whom you've been seeing on a consistent basis for more than six months. At this stage, you're basically dating and very used to each other—so much so that when someone amazing comes along and asks you out, you may feel reluctant to accept because of an obligation you feel towards your Niche Player. Perhaps you pass on the date and tell yourself, *He isn't my type* or *I'm just too busy with work.* We can fool ourselves into believing anything if we try. But this is a classic case of blocking yourself from major love potential, which happens frequently when you're hanging with a Niche Player.

2. *Easy & Convenient*

During my early college days, I met a woman I'll call Pamela. We had the same business major. We took a lot of classes together and became friends and casual lovers. We studied together and ended up doing a lot of social things. Before I realized it, we were a couple. She didn't hit everything on my Top 5 List, but the convenience was there—always available, covered me on class notes, membership in the same business school clubs, and so forth. I had allowed the so-called rigors of college life—academics, fraternity life, and career planning—to make it too difficult to play the field with the ladies on campus. But after two years of being with Pamela, I realized that I was doing what was safe and convenient. She wasn't a good match for what I needed and wanted in a relationship. This arrangement prevented me from being available to search for my perfect love match. I'm not saying Pamela wasn't an amazing woman. She could have made a lot of men happy, but I wasn't one of them.

> **- W -**
> Don't let the booty or the pecs distract you from what you need in a partner. I know, easier said than done.

You may be in your sixties and spend most of your time at home where you're most comfortable. Let's say you also live in a small private development, which minimizes the amount of people around you on a regular basis. Maybe you've been fooling around with your 250-pound, next-door neighbor who can't even hold a conversation . . . but it's easy. Heck, all you have to do is walk a few feet to get your sexual needs met. Perhaps, this is more out of convenience than a true romantic connection. In this example, I would suggest having fun for a few weeks and then moving on—even if you think there aren't any other options. *Don't let "easy" allow you to settle for less than you deserve.*

3. *Looks Good*

While working for a firm in San Francisco, I met a very attractive lady named Grace from the accounting department. She had the curves and the nerves. She made heads turn 360 degrees. Every Friday, many of us at the office would meet for happy hour to reflect on the week and allow the traffic to dissipate before making our commutes home. During one of these sessions, Grace and I had our first chance to get to know each other. It was difficult to keep my eyes from focusing on her great legs. At some point, the conversation quickly turned to exchanges about our individual sexual interludes in various parts of the city. My Playa instincts kicked in. And during next Friday's happy hour, we were at a local hotel having our own hot, one-on-one happy hour. These interludes expanded to midweek sessions where we would alternate covering the room costs. She was captivating, but when the physical activity and steamy conversations ended, we had nothing else. When she had a spare moment, she was on the phone with a family member or friend. It was easy to understand, since she was married with two kids. Our affair was about one thing: sex. Grace looked good to me, and I looked good to her. There were great mutual benefits. We hit it hard until it was time to let go. When the time came to end it, there wasn't any emotional stuff. We hugged, gripped each other's booty, then turned and walked away. What we had, we had. We both knew what it was without any confusion. This is what makes a Stand-In perfect. But unless you both accept the same terms, nothing good will come out of it. There will only be drama.

4. The Friend

We've all had one. For me, it was a lady I met through a friend. We always saw each other at social functions and started hanging out like pals. She seemed like a nice person, someone you could depend on, a person you could trust. She was always there for me. She even knew about some of my dating interests and listened to my critiques of the women I was dating. She had a warm presence and was a great companion at company functions. Our intimate encounters were never planned. They were pleasant and good. But there was one important problem: The relationship didn't have the "It Factor." Nothing knocked my socks off when I was with her, but she was always there for me. She hung around because she expected me to snap out of it and discover her as a perfect match. I felt awful when I had to tell her it wasn't going any further.

These relationships usually feel bad in the end, but it's better for both people when they're shut down. She deserved to be with a guy who cherished and loved her in the way she desired. I simply wasn't willing or wanting to do that.

Lauren's List

1. *Play Thang*

These folks are the ones you find at a club or whose phone numbers you have stored in your phone for late-night "emergencies." You don't spend time talking about anything serious whatsoever. All you do is meet, hook up, and go about your business. They are there strictly to fulfill your physical and sexual needs. Perhaps you have a drink down the block or play cards at your apartment before getting down to business, but that's where foreplay hopefully leads. You have no desire to get to know anything about him or her and wish to keep it that way. When you're on the brink of going crazy over not releasing all of that built-up tension in your body, all you have to do is pick up the phone or yell across the hall and, within minutes, all is right with the world. A Play Thang knows how to come right to the rescue in these situations.

> **- L -**
> Don't send flowers to or buy gifts for a Filler. It sends the wrong message. Save it for a real relationship.

In college, I had a Play Thang who was conveniently just down the hill from my dorm room. She'd walk up or I'd walk down so we could spend the night hooking up. It was fun, lighthearted, and consistently drama-free. I didn't even know her major, but that's how we both wanted it, even though those words were never said. We knew what kind of relationship we had and there was no confusion or fighting. After about a month and a half, it fizzled when we both went on Christmas vacation. But hey, it was great for what it was.

A fling with a Play Thang usually lasts a few weeks to several months until you want to move on to a new person. In this situation, we both got bored and it was over shortly after it began.

2. *Good Timer*

This is a person who is fun to be around and totally cool, but doesn't spark your interest or ignite a passion. You two are able to go anywhere and laugh, snuggle, and even talk about intimate things. But when it comes down to it, you don't feel a strong romantic connection. Does this mean you should be friends? Well, in a way you are, but not really since you occasionally get touchy and feely. Does this mean you should date? No way. You may have an awesome time for a night or day, but then you're ready to go back to your life and not think about him or her. After you get your fix, which takes just about that amount of time, you always go back to feeling like he or she just isn't right for you.

I have a lesbian friend who has had a Good Timer in her life for more than ten years. The Good Timer lives in Texas and my friend lives in California. Sometimes, when they are in between relationships, they hook up for the weekend and go to strip clubs or gamble. My friend always tells me how much fun they have together and that their connection is good. I always ask her, "So, why don't you try to be together?" She usually says something like, "I dunno, we just don't fit. I care a lot about her, but not enough to do anything about it." For them, they are comfortable with hooking up a few times a year and leaving it at that. Who knows if they'll end up together, but they're happy with the terms they've established.

3. The Ex

I'll admit that fooling around with an ex-lover probably isn't the best idea, but sometimes it feels great when you're single and lonely. Of course, it also depends on the two people involved and how the relationship ended. If things ended on a decent note and there is mutual respect and understanding, I say go for it. And yeah, I get it, the feelings are probably still there sometimes and you may rethink whether or not you both made the right decision to end things. So what? Life's too short to worry about that.

If you're still madly in love with an ex-partner, then being intimate on any level is NOT a good idea.

I've been known to be uptight and a major over-thinker. You know the person who takes forever and a day to make a decision? Yeah, that's me. And when it comes to love, I am even slower (if that's possible). So, when I started fooling around with one of my ex-girlfriends, I was just as shocked as everyone else. Me, the person who tells everyone, "Never sleep with an ex lover." Yeah, well, that's what I recently did for several months. I was living in the moment and getting my needs fulfilled. In the end, it didn't work out. However, I did get the closure I needed.

Was fooling around with my ex-girlfriend a bad idea? Could it have ended badly or with one of us hurt? The answers are probably yes and yes. Still, when you're single, you have the right to not think and do things that may just be stupid in the end. Hey, at least you had a good time doing it.

A word of caution: It will feel great to reconnect with an ex-partner and you'll probably want to get back together after a while. Pass on that. Remember that *you broke up for a reason.* Sure, sometimes it works out after you've both matured and been apart for a while. However, in most cases, the things you hated or the problems you had will resurface, and you'll be very disappointed in the end.

4. *Not Serious*

These types are usually very annoying because they pretend to be serious but don't back up what they say, such as, "I'd love to go out with you, but I have to spend the entire month with my lonely grandma." Now, if his grandma were actually ill, that would be a different story, but loneliness doesn't cut it. Not Serious tends to say everything just right, but blows it on a consistent basis, such as, "Hey, let's go out sometime next week." Yet, you never get a phone call or text message when that time comes. There is simply no follow-through with this type.

> - L -
> If the words don't match the actions, you've got a Not Serious on your hands.

However, that doesn't mean you can't make that person a Filler. You can take your relationship for what it is, which is an occasional good time. But be careful not to get your hopes up with Not Serious—this isn't easy, since he or she is the type of person you would date if they just kept their word. Constantly remind yourself: "She or he will never change." Be real with yourself. If you can't do this, then don't make Not Serious a Filler. You'll probably just end up getting hurt.

When It's Time to Move On

It's hard to know when it's time to close the door on your Niche Player or Play Thang. The key symptom to look for is *routine* and a feeling of *going through the motions.* A Filler should be fun and positive, not the opposite. When you're used to being around someone, it becomes easy to forget that you don't have to be around that person if you don't want to be. That's why it's critical to remember that you can come and go as you please without any explanations. At least that's how it should be. If not, then you're in a relationship with the Stand-In and it's really time to move on.

Though it may be hard to admit, some of you have even forgotten your Top 5 List and lost track of the fact that you're looking for a long-term relationship. No worries. It's very common and easy to do when you're busy with life and feeling like you're not getting the emotional intimacy you need. But don't saddle up with a *compromise companion—* just find a guy or gal who is cool and convenient and reflect on your next moves. Remember to keep yourself out there.

Chapter Summary

It's important to ask yourself what kind of Stand-In you want and why. If it's for emotional reasons, then you probably want a relationship and should consider remaining alone and focused on waiting for your perfect match. Yeah, this can be hard, but it's worth the wait. And for those of you looking for a deep emotional connection, you're better off skipping the Stand-In. You may be subconsciously turning away a great love interest by spending so much time with a Filler. These situations seem easy to avoid until you're involved in one. Wait and, eventually, The One will come. For the time being, isolate your attention on friendships and family time.

Also something to keep in mind is, some people cannot be intimate without getting emotionally attached, and that's okay. That's why you can't count on the Good Timer to blossom into the perfect love match for you. Keep your Top 5 List pinned to your underwear to keep you on focus. We're kidding, but you get the idea.

William's Old School Wisdom	Lauren's New School Wisdom
There's nothing wrong with casual dating. Just know what you want, because you aren't getting any younger.	Know what kind of Filler you have and make sure you're both on the same page.
Play the field and put yourself out there. You'll like the new experiences.	If you're a young person, consider having a temporary Filler. Relationships can be distracting and you may need to consider not being in one.
Don't get too comfortable with Stand-In dates. They will block you from meeting your perfect match, and they will burn precious time off the clock.	If you're consistently avoiding relationships over a very long period of time, it may be time for some counseling.
Staying in the present will make you complacent. Keep your focus on the game and your ultimate goal.	If friends judge you for having a Stand-In, tell them to back off. It's not their business or place to do that, even if it comes from a place of concern.

8.
The Big "C"

You may be at the finish line, but the race ain't over.

If you're dating someone and have reached this chapter, things are getting very serious. Your heart is invested, your sweetie knows you on an intimate level, and you guys are starting to feel like taking the dating relationship to the next stage. Yeah, it's no joke.

You are now way past the first round of the Playoffs and quickly approaching the Finals. From the work you've done in earlier chapters of this book, you know that your Boo has satisfied the Top 5 List requirements, shown no major Red Flags, and met most of the important people in your life. Also, the two of you are on the same page about the future and your feelings for each other. At the end of the day, there shouldn't be anything stopping you now from taking home that trophy we like to call The One.

Some of you have been seeing your Boo for several months, while others may be going on several years. It doesn't matter how long it has been. You'll know when everything simply feels right in your heart. What does it mean when *everything feels right*? We'll get to that in a moment.

In this chapter, the focus is on embracing the Big "C": **Commitment**. We'll talk about what the Big "C" really entails because it's so important that you're on the same page as your partner. Since you may be way past the six-month mark, it's important to clarify how committing makes the relationship different. We also want to shed light on things you might not have thought about, in order to ensure that you're making the right decision. Sure, we're getting sort of protective on ya, but it's only because we want the best for you and your heart.

Some people are Big "C" *Cravers* and others are Big "C" *Escapers.* If you have a history of jumping too quickly or yearning to settle down, you are a Craver for sure. If you always pull back when things get too close, deep, and emotional, you are an Escaper. For those of you who have identified yourself as one of these types, no need to panic. Knowing what you are is the biggest hurdle. It's the people in denial who need to get real, because that unwillingness to see the truth can negatively impact a dating relationship. In other words, it can end it—pronto.

We want to highlight some things to help you identify whether or not you have solid ground to walk on before heading toward the Big "C." **William**: Lauren and I both have different requirements, but having them is what has helped both of us in our own dating situations, and continues to help Lauren.

Let's Break It Down
It has to feel right

William: This is not an analytical exercise to assess your situation. No. You get to this point after several months or years of building a solid relationship. After dating my **wife-to-be** (Jennifer) for several years, I realized everything **felt right**, which was not a feeling I was used to in other serious relationships. My **happiness and contentment being with her was obvious and natural.**

William's Big "C" Requirements

Being with Jennifer was different in many ways. It was a new experience for me. It almost felt uncomfortable. There were no arguments. Compromises felt good. We loved doing all kinds of stuff together. She gave me a different way of thinking on certain day-to-day challenges. Wow. But did I want to give myself completely and possibly get burned? No. So, I took some extra time, but the answer was the same: it felt right, I was content, and my mind was in a happy place.

Feels right + contentment = happiness

Here's what it came down to for me to ultimately give in to Jennifer.

> ➤ *We had love and friendship.* When I needed someone to talk to or get some steam off my chest about work, she would always be willing to listen. And the great part was, she would still have an open ear even when I was worked up or said something rude. Unconditional love is rare to find, and we found it. Unconditional love means you can say something stupid and that person still adores you.

> | - **W** - |
> |---|
> | If you're afraid of how intense your feelings are with the person you're seeing, still open up. Just do it at a slow pace like I did. |

> ➤ *It never felt forced.* It was never a struggle doing things and sharing our feelings. I could tell her about my hopes and dreams, such as pursuing a golf career or starting to sculpt art, and she could tell me hers, like being around animals and wanting to swim with dolphins. None of this was something we had to force. Negative energy didn't exist. Disagreements were minimal and short-lived. We easily talked through things and came to a mutual understanding and compromise. No passive-aggressiveness.

> ➤ *We complemented each other.* In the movie *Jerry McGuire,* the best line in the film is "You complete me." Where she lacked, I was strong, and vice versa. She's a quiet type who hates competition, and I thrive on it. When I'm riled up, she is the calm and collected voice who gets what she wants through simply being patient.

> ➤ *Open and honest.* We didn't hold back and never lied to each other. No one in this world is perfect. When I made mistakes, I owned up to them, and so did she.

Honesty and openness made our relationship stronger and brought us closer.

➤ *Mutual priorities.* We enjoyed being each other's caring and supportive partner. We were both focused on work and family. I had kids going into the relationship and she was supportive and a great mother figure to them. This is because we were on the same page about our priorities.

➤ *Marriage didn't change the relationship*, it only formalized it. Tying the knot only drew us closer. We knew it was the right decision and the seriousness of the action didn't scare us in the least since we felt so strongly about one another.

Close the Deal

Feelings regarding marriage apply to couples in serious dating relationships who are potentially ready to *close the deal.* I have old school values, so it was my goal to have a Soul Mate to share my life's journey. I believe two special people should eventually be joined in marriage or civil union once achieving the Big "C." Simply living together means you can bounce any time there is a problem or when you find someone better. This is not commitment.

But some of you always run away from the Big "C." You know you're not emotionally ready to go down this path. That's fine. Half of all marriages end in the Big "D" (divorce). Pulling back early is less painful than breaking it off later.

Let's Break It Down

Marriage + young = heck no

Lauren: To be real, what my dad is saying is very foreign to me. I haven't gotten to this point in a dating relationship, but it sure sounds hot. I can't help but feel like this is extremely hard to achieve as a young person. I know it's possible, but it sure takes a lot of effort and time, particularly if you're working hard on your career. Does this mean **we're bad people for wanting to keep the focus on ourselves**? I don't think so, since relationships heading for the Big "C" take time, money, and compromise. If you're not at a place where you can deliver those goods yet, it's okay.

Lauren's Big "C" Requirements

> *Not a lot of pressure.* This is critical to think about at every stage of dating, particularly during the Big "C." There's nothing worse than a guy or gal who is always expecting something of you, like getting a high-paying job or wanting you to finally tell your mom to stop calling every day. Over time, this will cause resentment, secrets, and discomfort. One time, I dated a woman who was not digging the fact that my profiles were posted on a few dating websites. She felt like I should have deleted all of them when we started hanging out. So, I deleted them right around the time our relationship transitioned into the Big "C." But after that, I felt like she was watching my every move and conversation, even if I was simply talking to a girl from work. I always felt a huge pressure on my shoulders, back, and everywhere in between to live up to her high expectations when I probably should have been more focused on why she wanted to be good friends with her ex-girlfriend so badly. I'm sure it's not surprising that within several

> **- L -**
> You should definitely delete all dating profiles if you're seriously digging the person you're dating.

months we grew apart. We just didn't trust one another. We broke up, and it wasn't pretty. Only one thing might have changed the outcome of this relationship, which I'll cover in my next requirement.

➢ *We're good friends.* Friends have trust, understanding, and tons of fun (at least most do). You both make mistakes without judgment and accept each other for who you are. In order for the Big "C" to blossom to its true capacity, a friendship has to be there. Without it, small things run the risk of ruining a great love thang. When I was dating the exotic dancer, I was unemployed and broke for the first time in my life. Plus, all I could seem to focus on was the fact that she was dancing for a living. It messed with my head and, as a result, I wasn't focused on truly getting to know her. I always told people we broke up because we were too different. I truly believe, however, that a lot of it was due to the fact that we didn't have the acceptance and understanding that two friends have.

➢ *We're both focused.* I'd really pay attention to this one if you're under thirty-five. When you're young and focused on your career, it's a good idea to consider being with someone who has the same mindset. Going into the commitment arena with a chick or fella who doesn't have any motivation will only hold you back as well. This won't have as much impact on two fifty-somethings since they both have some kind of foundation already established. However, peeps just starting their adult lives are in the process of building that foundation. The last thing you want is someone coming in and turning a masterpiece into a thousand useless pieces.

➢ *I can see a long-lasting marriage down the road.* Let's be super-duper clear: I'm not saying you want to marry the person right now, just that you can see yourself with this person for the rest of your life. And that the thought of marrying is a nice one, not one that makes you feel tied down and unhappy. Take a moment to reflect. Have you ever dated someone you loved but, deep down, you knew there was no chance of being in a successful marriage? Some of you might be in this situation right now and don't know what to do.

A friend of mine—I'll call him Charles—was dating a woman who was perfect for him on paper. She was smart, motivated, cute, loyal, and caring. The only thing missing was that Charles didn't feel like she was The One. Whenever we'd have conversations about her and where the relationship was headed, he'd say, "I'm not in love with her, but what are the chances of finding a chick who will treat me the way she does?" Charles might have been right, but they both deserved better than just rolling with the punches.

Settling is like gambling at a casino: you're going to get screwed at some point.

➢ *Without a doubt in my mind, I feel loved.* This is something many of us don't really think about. Our focus is usually on other things, like how we can express our love to show how much we care about the person we're dating. But *you* matter as well. Have you thought about how much your lover cares about you, and in what ways he or she shows it? I'm not talking about a smile or a hug in the morning. That should be a given. When it comes to the Big "C," there should be surprise gifts and thoughtful actions happening everywhere. Why? Because you deserve that. If it isn't happening, then consider whether you want to move on with that individual. Even though I think what I'm saying is obvious, let me break it down: peace out if you aren't feeling the love.

What's the Difference?

Six-Month Mark vs. *Commitment*

We think it's critical to know how the Big "C" level of your relationship will be different from the first six months. Things can get blurry if there isn't clarification up front. We want you to be crystal clear as you make the decision to commit—or not to commit—to the new love in your life.

Where You Stand

Six-Month Mark
The two of you are *exclusively dating.* You are not talking to anyone else romantically, but know it's a possibility that you both may decide to stop seeing each other at any moment. However, you're not making any serious long-term plans, like moving in together. It's best to focus on being friends with each other rather than picking out an overpriced condo.

> **- L -**
> In terms of signing something with your new Boo, really take time to think about that. You may be able to reverse a bad boob job, but not your signature.

Lauren: Flirting with or dating other peeps shouldn't be going down. Honestly, I tend to go into relationship mode at this point, which is like shooting the ball with twenty seconds to go on the shot clock. Not good. So, being able to balance and maintain boundaries is essential to grabbing that win in the long run. Sure, call and talk every day, but don't share a phone plan quite yet.

William: Things are set in stone at six months, or somewhere around that time. You still have one foot in and one foot out the door. It's kind of like a game of poker—sometimes you're in and sometimes you're out. Even though you two may have discussed that things are going well, there are no *major decisions* being made that impact both of you.

So, it's not quite serious yet, but if you do something serious like adopt a new baby, it will be.

Commitment
You are only seeing each other and *jointly* making decisions about important matters that impact both of you, such as taking a new job, making investments, or creating a home together.

William: With serious relationships, your planning takes on a longer-term view. You can talk calmly about the future and how you plan to live your lives together. If you both lived in separate homes, you'll be figuring out at this stage how to combine them into one home or looking for something that suits both of you. If one of you is offered a job, then you both reach a decision by discussing the options.

Lauren: You don't make any decisions without the other person. Now it's about two minds, not just one. Pets are being bought, "your stuff" is now called "our stuff," and vacations are planned together.

Personal Things

Six-Month Mark
You are very private about certain things, such as family matters, health issues, or personal problems. Frankly, it's none of your Boo's business. If one of you has to deal with a personal issue, it's on that particular person to figure out, although there is concern and care from the other person.

Lauren: A few years ago I started dating a nice woman right after I filed for unemployment. On top of that, I had just moved into a studio with my college friend. Basically, we were sharing a large room. So, I definitely didn't feel comfortable having anyone over since there was no space. Did I tell the person I was dating how stressed out I was? No. I didn't feel like it was her concern and I wasn't comfortable sharing my problems yet. Also, it was important for me not to feel like I was placing a burden on her shoulders by going into my trials and tribulations.

William: This is a boundary that many people cross early into a dating relationship. It's a sad thing to hear when someone can't find a job or has to have surgery on a bad knee. But this time is about having fun and keeping things light. Leave the personal issues at the door. I know it sounds harsh, but it will only help you and the other person in the end.

Commitment
You tell each other what's going on in your lives, including your challenges and problems. When you are struggling with your boss and your career is in question, you have a sounding board, a cheerleader, and an advisor. You become each other's primary supporter and helper in times of need. There is a feeling that you're a team that can solve and survive whatever issue you're facing.

William: Back in the day, my girlfriend's parents were going through a divorce. Her parents were trying to pit her against each other. She was torn and in distress many days during the year-long ordeal. She couldn't believe they were splitting up after twenty-eight years of marriage, and the home she grew up in was about to be sold. My role was to make sure she didn't get caught in the middle by keeping her neutral and somewhat distant. This was hard work, but I cared. Her parents had to work it out; my girlfriend had to remember she had her own life to live and so did they (when the whole stinking experience is over, they are your parents and will love you just the same). By being committed to her, I jumped on her emotional train and provided some conductor support.

Lauren: You two are in it to win it, no matter what happens. If one of you gets sick with mono or a bad flu, the other person is there to bring soup or whatever you need. In addition, there is an emotional support system that should be there. Nothing is too serious to be handled.

Decision Making

Six-Month Mark

You can make impulse decisions and there's no long conversation needed, such as suddenly flying with your best friend to Hawaii. You are not tied down, although you wouldn't go on this trip with an ex. That's a no-no.

William: Doing spontaneous things with other people, without your Boo, is not cool. When I look back, each time I did this it confirmed one thing—either my girlfriend was not that important to me or I wasn't ready to seal the deal.

Lauren: I have to disagree with my dad on this one. At this stage, I think it's cool to do spontaneous things with your friends. Why should you have to check in with your new lover to see if it's cool to spend the night in Vegas with your best friend? I'm not saying you just leave and don't let him or her know. You still keep the communication open and honest, as usual, while maintaining boundaries and your independence.

Commitment

If you go anywhere, even if it's just a day trip with your dog, you tell your Boo. You communicate your schedules and appointments about everything. No exceptions.

William: This has nothing to do with getting approval. It's simply about showing consideration for the other person. We're not just talking about taking trips to another city. It includes going out to lunch with an old high-school friend or meeting your golf coach for a lesson.

Lauren: You definitely have to tell your special somebody about that trip you've wanted to take to Vegas with friends. Before any plans are made, you need to get the green light.

Ex-Lovers

Six-Month Mark

If an ex is constantly messaging you on Facebook, it's not necessary to mention it. You can easily deal with that on your own in a mature manner.

William: People who let ex-lovers or flings come in and out of their lives are hurting themselves in the long run. You need to take steps to put a stop to this kind of lingering behavior. Their time is over. What you had, you had. So take care of it on your own without involving your new Boo.

Lauren: Telling someone that you're getting messages from your previous partner when you've only been seeing each other for a few months is a huge turn-off. It comes off as chaotic and desperate. Plus, it doesn't concern the person you're seeing. I've never been in this situation, but if I were dating someone who brought this drama onto the scene, I'd be concerned.

Commitment

You immediately mention when someone tries to make a serious move on you in a romantic way, such as an ex-husband. You have no fantasies about others or allow flirting in your game.

William: Communicating when there has been an inappropriate move made on you by someone like a previous partner or ex-wife or husband is essential. You never want to keep that quiet because it can come back to bite you. That person can fabricate the situation and make it seem like you were the one who made a move. The most important thing is your behavior and actions that prevent this from happening in the future. Cover yourself and communicate out of respect for your new Boo as well.

Lauren: You don't have to mention when a homeless person or stranger yells, "Nice booty!" However, if the mother of your kids or someone you were in a relationship with for several years tries to holla at you, that's information to communicate to your lover.

Meeting the Godfather or Godmother

Six-Month Mark

You've met a few select friends and family members in your lover's life. You might have met his or her mom or dad, but you haven't been to the family reunion yet.

Lauren: I used to let everyone meet my family, even if we had only been dating a month or two. Now I wait until we're in the Big "C." The downside is that it takes a while for my

Boo to meet my loved ones. The upside is that if things don't work out between us, they're saving a lot of time—and so is my family.

Commitment

At this stage, you know everyone who means something in your Boo's life. You've definitely met all of his or her friends, as well as their immediately family, more than a handful of times. Nothing should change between the two of you during these encounters.

William: My best buddy, Chris, was in a serious relationship with a lady named Veronica. They were a great couple. One day he told me he had never met Veronica's parents and relatives. Damn, this was strange, since they had been together for two years. Just think about all those holidays, vacations, and special events. Why? She was from a working-class Irish-American family and he was a professional African-American. Her father was against interracial dating, so she kept her relationship a secret from her family and friends. Terrible way to live. Chris hung in there for another two years before he realized she valued her family's feelings more than fully committing to the relationship. He ended it.

Let's Break It Down
Say goodbye

Lauren: The Big "C" is no joke, especially when you're a *young person*. Think long and hard about this. *Gone are the days you can go away for a day*, week, or month to Mexico or wherever and not have to tell anyone that you made out with a stranger. *Think of yourself as a ship* and your new lover as the *anchor*. You're now committed, which is a great thing if you're *happy*.

Questions to Ask Yourself

We love questions and think there's huge value in seeking out the answers, particularly when it relates to committing.

Yes, it's that time again. Get out that pen, iPad, or whatever you want to keep track of your thoughts.

For the *Old(er) Schoolers*:

- ➢ Is my new love as focused on family as I am?
- ➢ Does she or he support my kids and have a positive relationship with them?
- ➢ When we discuss marriage, does she or he have any hesitancy or reservations?
- ➢ How are we handling individual assets? Does it seem too complicated trying to keep things separate, or to consolidate?
- ➢ Is there any drama with an ex-husband, ex-wife, or previous partner?
- ➢ Can we easily come to a compromise during disagreements and move on?
- ➢ Do I think she or he would be there for me during an illness or tragic accident, or hit the road?

For the *New Schoolers*:

- ➢ Will moving in together distract me from my career or make me feel uncomfortable?
- ➢ Do I mind having to check in with my Boo if I want to go on a trip with friends?
- ➢ Can I see myself wanting to get married to and possibly start a family with this person?
- ➢ If he or she were offered a job in another country, would I be willing to relocate?
- ➢ Does the thought of committing seem strange or make me feel happy?
- ➢ Is there unconditional love between the two of us?

We want you to be absolutely sure about heading into the Big "C." Answering these questions should help you to feel even more secure about settling down with your new love. If the questions bring up concern for you, then take some time to think about the relationship. Talking to a close friend or family member may be a good idea as well.

Now What?

Assuming you are eating this stuff up and all systems are go, where do you go from here? If it's that good, you better put a ring on it. Don't waste time. The person you're with is a definite keeper, and they won't stay single forever.

If you're still wondering if the Big "C" is for you, don't worry. This person could still be The One, but you may still need some time to get to know each other. Try not to panic and assume the two of you aren't right for each other. However, if things aren't improving over time and nothing seems easy, don't ignore that. You two may not be a good match.

Chapter Summary

Be clear in your mind about what the Big "C" means and how it takes your dating relationship to another level. Remember that things are intensifying as you move past the sixth-month mark. Now you're living in a city called It's Gettin' Serious.

For those Big "C" Cravers and Escapers, listen to your gut and always keep things honest with your Boo. Communication is critical. Without it, two people can end up on different pages in a book that began as a great read.

If you have read this book up to this point, you are probably a Big "C" Craver. You sincerely want to be in a committed relationship. That's cool. Once you get out of your cave (if you have one) and get past the six-month mark with someone, don't be afraid to take it to the Big "C." There is risk in everything we do. Even when romance ends on a bad note, we learn something about ourselves. But it would be a mistake to shut down and retreat into our comfortable cave or make our Top 5 List impossible to achieve. Nope, accept outcomes for what they are, but stay in the game.

William's Old School Wisdom	Lauren's New School Wisdom
Friendship and commitment go hand in hand.	If you're young and career-driven, avoid marriage at this time.
It may take a while to find your Soul Mate, like it did for me, but it's worth it. Don't settle.	As you and your honey enter the Big "C," clearly explain your expectations and needs to each other.
Don't force it; it must come naturally. You must achieve an easy state of happiness.	Make sure you're ready to commit.
Take the time you need to get to the Big "C." It's more dangerous to be a Craver than an Escaper. But neither one ends up in a happy ending.	If you're a Big "C" Escaper, stay calm and don't run. The worst thing you can do is push away an amazing person because you're scared.

PEEPS ON A BUDGET
How to Advertise Yourself

Brought to you by Lauren

I've often mentioned how much I support dating websites as a way to meet people. However, it can get expensive and hard to filter out the good versus the bad without face-to-face interaction. So, what's the middle ground?

Meeting people starts with one thing, which doesn't cost you a dime:

❖ **A good attitude.** Ever read *The Secret*? Its main message is that we all have the power to attract what we desire, as long as we believe and use positive thoughts. If you need $70 for a subscription to Match.com, ask the universe. Suddenly your boss may ask you to pick up a shift or maybe you'll get an early birthday gift.

Here are some other tips for meeting singles:

❖ **Be on point at work.** Don't skip wearing makeup or showering for a few days because you think no one notices. Someone is always watching you.

❖ **Volunteer.** There are so many cute people who volunteer each week. You'll often find that they rarely go out to clubs since they're so busy with work and other obligations. This is good since you don't want a Clubaholic. By volunteering, you're doing something positive and getting to interact with the same individuals on a regular basis. It's a perfect way to get to know someone over time.

❖ **Be known as the Single Friend.** Don't be ashamed of being single—be proud. Tell all of your friends that you're single and looking. This can work wonders. My friend is a promoter, and when I go to her parties she always tells every cute woman that I'm single. It's great.

❖ **Have business cards on you 24/7.** Use them every chance you get. If you go onto Moo.com, you'll find great deals for inexpensive cards. Having them is a great way to give a dating prospect your information. Plus, it looks professional and like you have your shiznit together. Sexy.

❖ **Say "Sure" to everything.** Has your co-worker invited you to The Museum of Tolerance? You may not like museums, but say "Sure" anyway. Be open.

PEEPS WHO CAN SPLURGE
How to Advertise Yourself

Brought to you by William

Since your money is not funny, you have more resources and options available for getting yourself out there. Here are some things I recommend:

- ❖ **Appearance.** The billboard is you! Hire a style consultant and spare nothing on your clothes, skin, manners, and oral hygiene.

- ❖ **Online dating services.** The best ones have a membership fee and require some basic screening. I suggest joining two to three, each with a little different focus—e.g., looking for a serious commitment, fun or casual dating, international, religious, or activity-based relationships (sports, travel, and the like).

- ❖ **Join an *active* country club.** Surprisingly, there is a wide age group of singles who play golf or tennis and attend a club's social events. You can find fun people who are fit, intelligent, and financially secure.

- ❖ **College alumni organizations.** A mutual connection with your college can deliver easy introductions. You have common threads that bind, so use them!

- ❖ **Salsa dancing.** Join a dance group that meets at regular times each week. Learn how to salsa and tango. These people cut across all walks of life and professions. The positive and sensual energy is hot, too. Many of the groups travel to various cities to compete or just socialize and dance.

9.
Be Cool with Doing
You

Even Elizabeth Taylor had her rough days.

There are many people in the world who are doing their own thing and choosing to be single. Simply living life without going crazy is hard sometimes. And we know that dating isn't easy. It can be a daunting journey that some of you may not want to take at this moment, in the near future, or ever. But the most important thing is doing what makes you happy, remaining *positive*, and making sure you're always feeling cool. That in itself is a big achievement.

Perhaps, you're just out of a twenty-year relationship and think you'll never want to go out on another date again in your life. Maybe, the search for The One may be going on three years and your friends are pressuring you by constantly asking, "What's wrong?" We say ignore them. If you're okay deep down inside, then focus on yourself and do whatever brings on the coolness. Plus, the better you know yourself, the better you become at realizing what you want and don't want in a partner.

You are what matters most. *If you come away with just one thing from reading this book, it's knowing how important it is to listen to that little voice in the back of your mind.* It's cool if you decide to spend a lot of your time and energy on work and moving up in the field of your choice. Both of us have been there, whether it was in college (Lauren) or in the corporate arena (William). Only you get to make that call.

So the next time your friends give you a hard time for not having a date in a while, don't be afraid to say, "I'm doing something else tonight." They won't always understand or be interested in your business or other concerns. You don't need to apologize for focusing on yourself. Tell your homies, "I have a date with me tonight" if they get on your case for wanting to go home early after a girls' night out so you can finish that work project.

Nonetheless, you must constantly ask yourself whether or not you're drifting too far away from the action. "Me time" can quickly turn into isolation, which then becomes a Cave. At this stage of the journey,

> - W -
> We can give you enough advice to last a lifetime, but we can't find your Soul Mate. You gotta meet yourself halfway.

you want to strive for a great blend of work, family, play, and alone time. Being able to find happiness without having a romantic relationship in your life will eventually attract an ideal dating match. There's truth in the words, "When you aren't looking, love slaps you smack dab in the face."

Love Won't Come A-Knocking

However, if you've read this book and still feel no desire to get out of your isolated world or change your set ways to meet someone new, then **don't think that love is going to come knocking at your door.** You're better off returning this book and getting your money back. We don't want you to come away thinking, "Well, this was a good read" without actually putting your best foot forward and making an effort to improve. In order to see change, you have to want change. If you haven't tried a few of the exercises or ideas we've suggested and are left wondering why you don't see a difference in your love life, please be real with yourself by seeing that you haven't truly made a wholehearted effort.

How do you know if you're in this boat? Well, we have some questions for you.

> ➤ *How many times have you hit up that hot new club you've been meaning to check out with a few friends?*
> ➤ *Is the book next to your bed still your best friend or have you made an effort to put it down and try to focus on attracting a new love?*
> ➤ *Are your legs still hairier than Chewbacca's?*

The One-Stop Shop

William: I view companionship as a natural and fulfilling way to travel life's journey. I like having someone by my side to enjoy the ride with, so to speak. But everyone has different times in their lives when this urge becomes a priority...or not. Waiting for the right person is *cool.* Getting your mind in the right place is *cool.* Comparison-shopping is *cool.* Testing the goods first is *cool.* Going to the picnic alone is *cool.* Backing off when things are getting too crazy is *cool.*

> - W -
> Beware of *Confirmed Bachelors.* They love being single and don't want to settle down anytime soon, even if they say otherwise.

    Back in the day, a lot of my buddies wanted to stay single; the term back then was *Confirmed Bachelor.* Their lives involved hitting the clubs weekly, lots of house parties with an abundance of ladies, and Quick Hits followed by boy-to-boy bragging. Today, we simply lump them into the Playa category. "Yeah Dawg, you know what I'm saying!" If you don't know much about Playas, that's what they often say to each other.

    One night out in Los Angeles, I saw an old Playa friend of mine, Graham. At this point he was in his early fifties. It wasn't fun watching him across the club trying to work the room, dressed a little out of sync, not keeping up on the dance floor, and still chasing the young stuff. Graham told me once that he loved "loose women." But there we were, twenty years later. At what point is it enough? Was he really that comfortable still living that way? You gotta know when to quit.

    So, what am I saying? Let me be clear. In my view, a lifetime without a Soul Mate is *not cool.* If you know someone like my buddy Graham, take a closer look. Why are they stuck in their *Solo Syndrome*? Sometimes, it's as simple as not being able to assess yourself. I missed an opportunity as a buddy to reach out to Graham and give him something to think about.

    When you are in a fulfilling relationship, your partner embodies a lot of things that make life cooler. That person should encompass what I call your *One-Stop Shop.* The *One-*

Stop Shop is your friend, lover, companion, cheerleader, sounding board, and, over time, a stabilizing influence. No, it's never perfect, and relationships require work and commitment, but anything worth something requires these things.

We all deserve to find a One-Stop Shop.

Giving Up Too Soon

Lauren: I remember a woman I'll call Kelly. One day she told me that she was going to either move back home, which was in another state, or stay in California. What determined whether she was going to move? Finding a job within a month. She prefaced this by saying, "I'm going to look nonstop for a solid month. Like, every minute will go to job hunting. I'm sure I'll find something, but if I don't, then I'm moving back with my grandma." She kept saying this the entire day, even texting me about it while I was at work. It seemed surprising to me since she hadn't looked for work the entire year I'd known her.

Yet, I was convinced. I remember thinking, *This sounds like a solid plan.* But, each day, she did nothing but watch television at home or ride her bike. In fact, it was more like the opposite of what she said she'd

> **- L -**
> What Kelly said about her reason for moving was a cop-out, and cop-outs are never cool.

do. She would apply for a job here and there, but not on a frequent basis. On top of that, she complained the whole time about how much she hated Los Angeles because the transportation system was whack. She clearly suffered from a negative attitude, and only she could fix that.

In the end, she never got a job. She texted me after only a week's time, saying: "No word on any jobs...I texted my grandma. I'm moving soon. A month probably." I wasn't surprised, although I was hurt and felt like she was taking the easy road out, but she had to do what was best for her.

We must put our best foot forward in order to find the things we want in life—and that includes a great dating match. Putting things off, like joining a dating website or talking to a guy or girl you like, can't happen anymore. Kelly made me see that we must, at times, **work hard for the things we want in life without throwing in the towel too soon.** Giving up without putting in your best, long-term effort isn't cool. If you keep telling yourself, "I'll try next month to find someone" without actually trying, then you risk ending up just as alone as Graham.

Cool vs. Not Cool

It can be confusing to pinpoint when we're going in the wrong direction in terms of "doing us," so here are some examples of situations that pass and ones that don't.

1. You've been working on a screenplay and it's almost finished. You're getting a lot of buzz and a big agent is showing interest, but he needs it within a month's time. Coincidentally, you've also met a great person who has asked you out on a first date. You agree, but then decide to postpone it until you're finished with the script.
SCORE: *Cool* **(Lauren);** *Not Cool* **(William)**

> **Lauren:** This is definitely *cool* and sexy because you're choosing to focus on your career and not give it up for anyone else. If I were dating someone like this, I'd be even more interested and would gladly wait.

> **William:** All work and no play! Bad, bad, bad. You can do BOTH. Have a little fun and get your mind off the project. When you return, you'll have a fresher perspective. The key is time management. Surely, you can squeeze in lunch, dinner, a movie, or whatever.

2. There's a hot new happy hour spot right around the corner that your co-workers keep inviting you to every week. You always tell them you have to go to the gym since you recently lost sixty pounds and want to stay in shape.

SCORE: *Not Cool*

> **William:** You are still thinking like an overweight person. Don't use the gym as an excuse. In fact, it sounds weird. You need to start showing off your new stuff. Just stay committed to weight control during happy hour. Those drinks can catch up to you and before you know it—bam! You'll have a couple four-pound twins called love handles.

> **Lauren:** It's so great that you lost a lot of weight, but not cool that you're using the gym as a reason to avoid going out. You could meet Mr. or Ms. Right at happy hour, but you'll never know since you'd rather run on the treadmill all night. Don't get me wrong, staying in shape is cool, but getting obsessive with it isn't.

> - L -
> Noticing an improvement in someone's appearance is a great conversation starter and makes the person feel great.

3. You met this great girl at the mall while looking for this book. You begin to talk and the next thing you know, you are having coffee together full of laughter and smiles. This chance, sixty-minute encounter leads to her calling you the following week to see what's going on this coming weekend. After exchanging pleasantries for a few minutes, you thank her for calling and end the conversation because the Lakers are playing the Celtics in a few minutes.
SCORE: *Not Cool*

> **William:** She is reaching out. This is a guy's dream. Are you insane? Call her back immediately and apologize for the quick conversation. Say you were in the middle of fixing a flat tire or something. Then, ASK HER if she wants to get together.

> **Lauren:** Wow, so not cool. I'm a huge fan of basketball, but there's no way I'd get off the phone to catch a game when my potential Soul Mate is on the

other line. DVR the dang game and chat for at least twenty minutes. This is plenty of time to schedule a date.

4. You have a co-worker named Jasmine and she is a ten plus. All the fellas, and some ladies, wish they were lucky enough to have her. After a long day working with her on a project, you get the nerve to ask her to have dinner that evening. She is touched by your offer and wants to, but has to pick up her five-year-old daughter at the daycare center by 6:30 p.m. **SCORE:** *Cool*

> **William:** This is a great opportunity to score some major points. Invite her and her daughter to join you for a quick bite. Why work hard all day and rush home to cook dinner? It's your treat, nothing fancy, plus it will be quick.

> **Lauren:** You definitely can't get mad at her for being a good mother, which is oh so cool. I don't think I'd go as far as inviting her and the little one over because it may mess with your daily routine (who knows how long they'll be there?), but I would definitely ask her what night works for her.

5. As a graduate student at one of the top universities in the country, you have limited time to do the things that matter to you the most. So you've decided not to be in a serious relationship until you've completed the program. **SCORE:** *Not Cool*

> **Lauren:** I'm all for being smart and responsible, but this is a little drastic. While attending New York University, I was in a study group led by Ryan, a teacher's assistant. At the time, Ryan was in a challenging graduate program and still managed to be in a relationship. Sure, he was a constantly disheveled mess and always complained about how

many eighty-page papers he had to write, but his game was clearly still on point.

William: There has to be balance in all areas of life. You can't have all work and no play, or vice versa. You'll end up unhappy and alone in the end. So put the books down once a week or twice a month and go out. The work will still be there.

6. You just got out of a four-year relationship a few months ago and love flirting with people, but nothing more serious than that. You feel like you aren't quite ready yet.
SCORE: *Cool*

William: Flirting never hurt anyone. You are single, have no one holding you down, and are probably enjoying the free life, even though your heart may be hurting for a while. It's all good. Luckily, *you can always flirt with a broken heart.*

Lauren: It's sexy when peeps know what they're ready for and what they should avoid. I'd hope the conversation would go something like this:

> You: "How's it going?"
> Woman: "Good, just got here. I've been waiting to have a drink all day."
> You: "What are you having?"
> Woman: "Um, before you get excited, you should know that I only want to flirt. I'm taking a long break from relationships right now."
> You: "Seriously? Dating, kissing, and sex are all out of the picture, too?"
> Woman: "For the time being, yup."
> You: "I feel you. Good luck."

Honesty is always better than withholding important information, such as still being in love with an ex-partner.

The Solo Syndrome

Those of you who are flying solo right now are split into two groups. One group is doing it the cool way with a great balance of going out, working, and having fun. The other group is alone out of fear or a sense of unworthiness. We've all been there before and know it can be a deep hole that's hard to escape from. Here are the symptoms of the Solo Syndrome.

Rejected and worn

You feel like no one wants to be with you after getting shot down a few times. You think love is possible, but you're just tired of not getting a "yes" from people you ask out.

Lauren: I can relate to this. I recently asked out a woman I thought was interested in me, but boy was I wrong. I said, "I like to be honest and open. I like you. Would you like to go out on a date with me?" Her response was, "You're great, but I'd like to focus on a creative friendship with you." *Sigh.* It hurt, but I still know how much I have to offer, and you should, too, if this happens to you. We have to remain positive and get back on that horse.

Thinking it'll never happen

The reason for thinking this can vary. Perhaps you've gained some weight or just ended your tenth failed relationship. So you spend your time in pajamas most nights fully believing that love will never come. *Just because it didn't happen in the past doesn't mean it won't happen in the present.*

Scared to be loved

Most of this is subconscious and should be dealt with in counseling. So let's focus on *actions.* When you see a hot man or woman approach you or smile, do you avoid making eye contact? Do you try to veer in the other direction? This is fear behind the wheel. Has someone amazing shown interest in you by offering to take you out whenever you're free, but somehow you've been too busy to follow up? Yup, that's fear rearing its head again.

If you've just identified yourself, consider making some major changes if you want to find that special somebody. We can't dictate what the specific changes are, as they're different for everybody, but we can be real by telling you: *the path you're on is not a cool one.*

> **- L -**
> Try re-reading the first five chapters in addition to doing the exercises. This may help.

Chapter Summary

To all of those operating solo right now in a cool way, stay strong. Your match is coming as long as you remain positive and visible.

To those still in a cave, what are you waiting for? Life is not a dress rehearsal. Let's get going. Stop eating alone so much and being glued to the TV watching *Oprah, Jon Stewart,* or reality shows. Maybe your hobbies have pulled you away from society at large. The most common reason people get stuck at this point is because they're discouraged. We've all been there. Hang tough. Remember, you are a quality person and your match is out there looking for you, too.

William's Old School Wisdom	Lauren's New School Wisdom
Be comfortable doing you—but don't let it turn into a Cave! Make sure you have balance.	Always be positive. It becomes contagious.
Be selfish with your time. Don't waste it on compromises just because your friends insist. Protect your priorities from distractions.	Young peeps: If you go out 24/7 after work, try *being cool doing you* by staying home a few nights a week.
Test the waters whenever possible. Be bold. What can it	Don't forget about your Visibility Menu. You may not

hurt? The worst thing you can get is a "no."	be focused on dating right now, but you should still be going out and be seen.
Stay positive and walk tall. Don't get down on your chances. You might be surprised at who is watching,	

10.
Scenarios

It's better to have a coat and not need it than to need a coat and not have it.

Here are a few *what if* situations that may help you on the dating scene. We've divided them by topic in relation to each chapter. We hope these scenarios will address any questions or concerns you may have that we didn't cover in the rest of the book. If you're still left with any confusion or uncertainty, shoot us an email. We're here for you.

Are You Living in a Cave?

A great guy has asked you out on a date, but between work and spending time with your two children, you can't figure out how to fit him into your schedule. Unfortunately, your ex-husband isn't around to help watch your kids, and you can't afford a babysitter. As a woman in your thirties, you still want to go out every now and then, but you feel stuck. What do you do?

William: I was a single parent and had limited finances at one point. The most important thing is having a support system, i.e., a friend or relative who can cover for you periodically for evenings out. For other times, look at creative ways to meet up, such as having lunch when the kids are in school or busy with other activities. But for serious relationships, after the first couple of dates, he needs to be exposed to your "real" world at home. Why? You are a package deal—you and the kids. He has to accept the total package, period.

Lauren: First of all, whatever you do, don't take your kids out on a date with this man. That's a bad idea and will put them and him in a very unfair situation.

Now that we're past that, let's break it down. You're young, but starting to climb up there in age. Time is not your friend. Plus, this guy is looking like a great male figure who could potentially be in your kids' life one day. You don't want to blow it with him by waiting a month to get a day off of work or to find a friend willing to watch the kids for a night.

I think the first thing to do is have a short "pre-date" during your lunch hour, or right after work before you go home to your family. I only say this because you have kids and you don't have time to waste—like an entire night—figuring out if this guy is a candidate or not. A pre-date will give you all the information you need to answer: "Should I go out with him?" You're a grown woman who knows what she's looking for at this stage in life, which is why the pre-date won't need to be longer than twenty-five minutes.

You're twenty-five and you work forty-five hours a week. On the weekends you want to have fun, but your friends seem to only want to get drunk or stay out too late. And frankly, you don't have the time or energy for that.

Lauren: This is a common problem that impacts many people like me: social, young, and fun, but at an awkward stage in life.

> - We're too young for older people to take us seriously, yet we're too old to take younger peeps seriously.
> - We want to drink, but we don't wanna get drunk.
> - Our careers are growing, but our banks accounts basically remain the same due to debt.
> - We want to go to the club, but we don't wanna close it down anymore.

In our closet, we divide our clothes into different sections according to the style, like pants, skirts, jackets, and so forth. The same goes for the peeps in your life. I would say to first make a list of categories in which your current friends fit. Some examples are "getting drunk buddies," "club buddies," or "close friends." Once you have your list and see where everyone is, you'll get an idea of what area of your buddy closet needs to be filled.

Next, I suggest you go shopping. Start making new friends on a different level by going to business networking events, college mixers for alumni, church, or spiritual workshops. I guarantee you'll meet some lovely peeps who know how to have fun and can carry on a nice conversation—well before your bedtime.

William: You have to be selfish with your time and interests. Don't just be a willing follower. Getting drunk should not be a common thing. If it is, you have an alcohol problem. People are not attracted to heavy drinkers or smokers. First, clean up your act and do things in moderation. Second, plan your weekends around the things you like to do and people to do them with. Third, set goals for yourself and make sure you are doing things to achieve them. Frankly, drifting through the weekends is not helping you achieve your goals in life; therefore, the fault rests on your shoulders. This is not the lifestyle of successful people.

What's Your Top 5?

You're twenty-five years old and recently met a really awesome woman at a political rally. The two of you exchanged numbers and had great phone conversations. Now, during your first date (which is going extraordinarily well), you find out that she has two kids and has no involvement in their lives. When you ask why she doesn't want to be a more active mother, she tells you that she needs to focus on herself right now. What should you do?

Lauren: I would feel uncomfortable dating this woman because she doesn't seem stable within herself or her life. Sure, it's understandable to go through hard times. We all need a little space every now and then. However, when major responsibilities fall to the wayside, such as kids, I begin to feel concerned. If ditching the kids is on her menu, then anything is fair game to be chewed up and spit out.

William: Red Flag. Refer to my Top 5 in chapter 2, item #4: "Shared Values." A parent who ignores their kids in this manner doesn't have enough heart, conscience, or family commitment to share my world. This lady is not responsible. It's all about her. However, if she is giving you good vibes, it's okay to give in to the moment and have a few intimate dates, but don't stay long enough to get sucked into her world and her agenda. Protect your heart and get out early.

As a forty-five-year-old man, you find extreme intelligence and maturity to be critical in the women you date. You recently met a great woman who shares the same values, is one of the smartest women you know, and always knows how to carry on a great conversation. There's only one thing you don't like: her lack of passion. She has a great job that she hates, and doesn't have anything that makes her excited in life. You don't know if it's your place to think about this or just to be thankful you found a woman who meets most of your needs.

William: As a middle-aged man, you need to look a little deeper into a relationship with this lady. If passion is a concern for you, this could be a Red Flag that kills the relationship long-term. Why? Because it is an important value she does not share with you. It would be worth investing some time seeing if you can help her rekindle passion in her life. For instance, you could try to engage her in one or more of your passions. Through your actions and energy, she might be willing to rethink certain things— family, career, social life, hobbies, and so forth.

You need to determine if this lady hits your Top 5 criteria. If so, you may be able to lead her to a more passionate place simply by being her new Soul Mate. If this is the case, you also have an opportunity to help guide her toward finding a career or job that is more exciting and fulfilling.

However, if she doesn't have anything that excites her, there is a deeper psychological problem, one that you cannot fix. Just being supportive isn't enough. Usually, people who have no passion also lack purpose and drive. They can be negative and drain your energy. Being with someone like this will simply bring you down. In that case, you need to move on.

Lauren: This is a tough one. If you just want to have fun or be in a short-term relationship, then go out with her. But if you're looking for more, then I would say stop dating her. If she's not motivated or passionate about anything in life, that will impact your relationship. It's also more than likely she won't be that passionate about you, either—or the two of you as a couple.

I've dated someone who didn't have a passion in life. She was negative and complained about this often, yet did nothing to change it. She had a lot of great qualities, but, in the end, I felt like I needed more. Since I am so excited and passionate about life and my dreams, it felt like she was holding me back. You want to be with someone who will make you a better person, not the opposite.

Caution Flags

For about a month now, you've been talking to someone you're really feelin'. Everything is great when you're face-to-face, but she only communicates through text messages outside of your weekly dates. What do you do?

Lauren: I say communicate with her about how you're feeling, whether it's confusion or just plain hurt. Everyone deserves a second chance, ya know? And then if shiznit doesn't improve, drop 'em like a hot plate and keep it movin'. If the communication is bad now, trust me, it won't get better.

William: Nothing beats live voice to live voice. Right from jump street, let the person know that you need to communicate mostly by phone and only text periodically. Maybe something is going on in her life and she is stressed or worried. Is she avoiding you? Is she shy and less talkative? Is she busy with work, kids, and the like? Is there a financial issue and she is managing her minutes? Whatever, it needs to be discussed.

There's a guy you like, but he has a strong body odor, particularly after he goes to the gym. You feel terrible for admitting it, but you feel like this is a deal breaker for you. Your friends are telling you that it's superficial to let him go over something so small. You don't know what to do.

Lauren: The first thing I want to say is: don't feel bad about your deal breakers. Your friends have them and so does the rest of the world. Some things, whether big or small, make us want to scream...and that's okay.

The second thing is: bad body odor *is* a big deal. Keep in mind that you're dating someone with the hope that he or she will be the person you'll marry. If I'm going to be with someone for a lifetime, they need to smell right. There's no way around that. I know it would get to me over time, no matter what I tell myself.

I say follow your gut and your heart. If they're saying you need to move on, then let him go in a nice way. Don't tell him, "You stink, so we're done dating!" Just politely tell the guy that you believe the relationship has run its course, although you think he's incredible. He'll understand and probably continue stinking up every place he enters. At least he won't feel self-conscious since you didn't make him feel bad for being himself.

William: An isolated "smelly" encounter can be explained easily. However, if we're referring to a daily body odor problem, that is serious. Don't let your friends say it's not. If it's constant, it could be attributed to poor hygiene, cultural divide, a health issue, or all of the above. My tolerance for people who have poor personal habits is zero. This is about as obnoxious as heavy smoking, obesity, or bigotry.

Red Flags

Sue is a twenty-six-year-old nurse. She met this guy George, a thirty-six-year-old high school football coach and the youth minister at a local church. He is considered a great guy and is highly respected in the community. George has never been married, but has had a few close calls. Sue and George started dating about a month ago and have a strong attraction to each other. However, on their last few dates, Sue discovered he was a heavy pot smoker and that he was doing the church job solely for the income and hated going to weekend services. What should Sue do?

William: Say goodbye. This guy is living a lie. His vice (smoking pot) is not acceptable, but more importantly, he is misleading church members and is a poor role model for the kids at his school. Major Red Flags. Sue uncovered all of this in the first month of dating. Wow, maybe there's more. This could get scary. Break it off now!

Lauren: As a young person, at first you may think the idea of a football coach and youth minister smoking pot is fun and interesting. It's probably not what you're used to seeing from someone who's older. But, then, it'll click that he's not a good role model. He's flat out lying in numerous ways. As a woman with a great job and a bright future, you must move on. At this age, you can't risk wasting time on anyone who will bring you down or distract you from excelling in every part of your life. This fool you met will do just that and more. Delete his number pronto.

You're a forty-two-year-old man with a great career. You've been dating a wonderful man around the same age for two months. Recently, he revealed that he has two kids from a marriage that ended five years ago. You ask why he didn't tell you before and he says, "I didn't want to scare you or make you question my sexuality." You can't believe he kept this a secret. However, part of you understands and empathizes since you were once married as well, though you have no children. What should you do?

Lauren: This is a tough call, but I think there are some deeper issues going on here that need attention. He may be going through a sexual identity crisis since he's blaming his lack of communication on being gay. In reality, telling you he has kids should have nothing to do with whether or not he is into men. Also, this makes me question his maturity level.

I would give it a few more weeks and be on the lookout for other Red Flags, which I think will come up soon. He sounds like a guy running away from himself. People like that always sabotage things in their lives, particularly if it's outside their comfort zone. Is it bad that he didn't tell you he has kids? Of course. But, I don't think you should stop seeing him just because of that.

However, if you're a twenty-something like me, run out of his place like there's a fire! You don't have time to deal with kids right now.

William: When it's early in the dating game, it's normal to hesitate about baring your soul until you are comfortable with the other person. But dropping a surprise like this on your new dating companion is serious and should cause you to wonder about honesty, openness, and lifestyle preferences. These are all normal reactions. If the sparks are still flying, you can continue dating with caution. Just keep your radar up and look closer to see if there are other surprises. If so, get out fast.

Slow Your Roll

You're twenty-eight and feeling fantastic after a recent job promotion. Now, your career is really moving fast, which is important to you. The girl you've been seeing for two months just told you she wants to quit her job because she's not happy and asks to move in with you for a while. What should you do?

Lauren: I think it's way too soon to talk about living together. She sounds like she's going through a hard time and may be looking for you to find her. Offer support while being honest about your boundaries. The fact is, you're taking care of yourself right now, which is what most young peeps must do. You have a lot at stake with your new job and can't risk being distracted by having your love interest constantly around.

William: Move in after two months? No way. It's too early and on top of that, having a new romantic roommate will kill the rest of your action. Why allow someone to move in and block your game, drag your finances down, and put heavy mental baggage on you? Plus, you're riding high with your new job promotion. Don't change anything.

Today's a big day. The guy you've been seeing asked you to marry him and it feels right. You've never felt this way in all of your forty years and want nothing more than to be with him. Yeah, only a few weeks have passed, but so what? This guy is The One, plus both of your kids get along very well.

Lauren: To be real, I don't know the right answer. My head and mind say, *Don't do it!* But then again, why not take a risk? So what if it doesn't work out? Yeah, you'll have a broken heart, but probably gain some awesome memories and have even more babies along the way.

William: This is what teenagers do. Slow things down and enjoy the great relationship you are experiencing. If it's that good, marriage two weeks into dating won't make it better. Go away for a long weekend to a romantic place and burn some of that energy. Quick courtships almost always end in divorce. It can leave you financially hurting, emotionally drained, and a lonesome, single parent.

The Six-Month Mark

You're twenty-seven years old and have been dating a great chick for the past few months. She's into your friends, loves watching sports with you, and even deals with your messiness. Lately, though, she keeps mentioning that she is good friends with her ex-boyfriend and often refers to their frequent conversations. You have previous partners in your life, too, but rarely speak with them. You don't know if anything is going on with your girlfriend and her ex, but it doesn't feel right. What should you do?

Lauren: You don't have time to waste on dating someone who insists on talking to her ex all the time. If you feel like she's absolutely worth it and that nothing is going on between the two of them, then talk to her about it. But regardless of her response, I think you'll still be bothered. That's why I say tell her you're not comfortable with them talking or having any kind of close relationship. If she refuses to respect that, then let the relationship go fast. From my experience, this issue is a big hurdle that most peeps can't jump over.

William: There is no right or wrong answer. Personally, I can't date someone who has a "close" relationship with her ex. If they are that close, why stop dating? Why can't they move on? I need undivided attention. If you have me in your stable, no other stallions are needed in the barn.

You're a fifty-five-year-old man and feel like you're falling in love with the woman you've been dating for seven months. There's just one thing you don't like about her. For a long time, she's been promising to be more interested in the things you enjoy, like hiking and going to museums. Yet, she isn't making any effort to do that. Also, she promised that she would come to one of your important art exhibits and didn't show up because she "suddenly had to work late." You don't know whether to end things or just continue to be patient.

William: There are too many fish in the sea. Drop it like it's hot. Sharing and enjoying each other's outside interests should be fun. If she bails with plenty of notice and blames it on work, she better produce some major evidence to keep herself in the game. She is selfish and is minimizing your world. Women need a *real* man, not a patsy who assumes the victim role.

Lauren: Wow, I would say get away from her as soon as possible. She's showing signs of selfishness, disinterest, and dishonesty. These are not good characteristics to be seeing so early into the dating relationship. I would highly consider having a discussion about how you're not happy and think you'd be better off as friends. Just think, if it's this bad now, how will it be a year down the road?

It's official. You're falling hard for this guy you've been dating for two years. He's charming, cute, friendly, kind, and focused. Plus, all of your friends love him. Dang, even your dog Lola likes him and she tries to bite you most days. You just don't like the fact that he's been unemployed for the past nine months. He doesn't ask you for money or complain about being jobless, yet this is an issue in your mind. If he's not that serious about finding a full-time job, then how serious can he be about being in a serious relationship down the road?

William: Maybe you can blame it on the recession. But having no job and having no desire to find one are two different things. It's important to know the full story. He might be a good guy who has just had a run of bad luck. If so, be patient and careful with your emotions and money. You may have a good guy who needs time to get back on his feet. But if he is happy with his lot in life, you need to move on, unless you like having a "kept man" in your crib.

Lauren: I think you need the entire story from him. Is he looking for a job or is he cool with being unemployed? When I didn't have a job, I wasn't cool with that. At the same time, I enjoyed the time off. However, I eventually made myself get out of my comfortable lifestyle and find work. If he's not motivated and doesn't care about changing things, then it's time to move on. If he does care, then stick by his side.

The Stand-In (Filler)

You broke up with your ex several months ago and you haven't spoken since. Recently, you were hanging out at a bar and ran into her. You both agreed to have a drink alone somewhere and talk. It was like old times and you had a lot of fun. The night ended with you two having sex. Things seem to be different and you find yourself wanting to try things again. It's a tough situation and you're wondering if it can work again.

Lauren: Been there, done that. Don't do it. Nothing good comes out of it. But, if you want to hook up, go for it. Hot, hot, hot.

William: *You* broke up for specific reasons. Don't forget it! In the moment, you can easily forget the bad stuff. And when there are no expectations, the pressure is off. Don't make the same mistake twice. You're smarter than that.

The Big "C"

You're in love, have wonderful friends, and feel that life is full of amazing opportunities. There's just one issue: You've been offered a job that, if you accept it, would make you have to relocate across the country. It's a great position, but you don't know what to do since it would impact your current dating relationship. Should you stay or should you take the job?

William: How long have you been in this relationship? Are you past the six-month mark? Are you both in discussions about the Big "C"? If you are not in a committed relationship yet, you should consider the out-of-town opportunity and see how it goes. You can always quit and move back if the relationship dictates or if the job doesn't work out.

Lauren: If you're fully committed and past the six-month mark, then you both should discuss what to do, whether it's move together or have a long-distance relationship. In terms of commitment, it's about two minds. Come to a decision together.

Pressure, pressure, pressure. That's how you feel about committing, no matter how much you want to be with the person you're seeing. Ever since you got your heart broken a handful of years ago, you can't seem to cozy up to the idea of fully giving yourself to another person. Part of you wants to, but a huge part of you is just too scared to risk getting hurt again. You fear that you'll clam up and sabotage things after you have the Big "C" conversation, which is why you've been avoiding it for more than eight months. Now is the time to decide what you're going to do...but you just can't figure it out.

Lauren: I can completely relate to feeling scared, but you can't let this stop you from going to the next step with someone you love. I would highly suggest counseling first and foremost, and then take it from there with professional help. This isn't a bad thing. You just need some support so you don't potentially ruin a great thing.

William: Who are you? Where are you at this point in your life? What are your most important priorities: career, hobbies, social causes, ultimate dating? Whatever it is, you are not ready for the Big "C" at this time. Why are you so paranoid about a close relationship? Was it because of a bad experience? One thing is for sure: you would benefit from a few therapy sessions. In the meantime, don't push your comfort zone, and get some professional advice.

You're a thirty-five-year-old man who is fully comfortable with yourself. Too bad you can't say that about the guy you've been dating. He hasn't come out to anyone in his life; in fact, they all think he's straight. After months of promising you he'd come out, it still hasn't happened. Since the age of twenty-five—and many experiences with men like this—you've told yourself you would never date someone who is in the closet...yet, here you are again. Should you wait or should you run as fast as you can?

William: I'd be stuck on the fact that he's been dishonest rather than not coming out, since that is his personal decision. He has to be ready to do that. However, you should have a discussion about the importance of sticking to what is promised. Stick it out, give him some time, and see what happens. If he doesn't follow through again, that's when you consider jetting. But you're committed now, so you have to be more patient.

Lauren: Coming out takes time and you can't force anyone to do that. You definitely have to wait for him to feel comfortable doing it. If you do it for him, he'll just be resentful and hate you one day. He may have promised you he'd come out because there's a lot of love between the two of you and he doesn't want to disappoint you. He's probably even tried to fulfill his promise, but whenever he gets the chance, he can't seem to do it. It's harder than we all think to come out. Be supportive and kind at this time. There's no deadline on this.

Be Cool with Doing You

Two years, three months, and twenty-three days. That's how long you've been single and it's getting old. All of your friends think you should stop looking for Mr. McAwesome and find a booty call since you're only twenty-four. But you don't have a problem holding out for that special somebody. If it takes five years, that's okay with you. That just means more time with friends and family in your eyes.

William: The main thing is being comfortable in your own skin and feeling good about your convictions. If you are really at peace with your current status, it's nobody's business. That said, it's important to have your eyes wide open and see the world and all that it has to offer. Holding out to find *perfect* might be hurting your chances of actually finding the *right* person. This is a form of the "living in a cave" mentality.

Lauren: Sure, do what makes you happy, but still put yourself out there by going to events and other places to remain visible. If you're with friends and family all the time, that kind of says you're using them to hide out. Find a balance. Make sure to go out and meet new people each week while remaining close to friends and family. You're young, so act like it.

It's hard for you to be alone. You don't know much about yourself, but you know that much is true. Every time you get out of a relationship, you jump into another, like now. This guy you've been seeing for a few months says he likes you a lot, but thinks you need time to be alone. You think this is crazy and can't even fathom doing this, but something inside of you thinks he's right.

Lauren: I would recommend being alone for a while. It will feel weird, but if you're hearing someone close to you say this, then it's time to take a look in the mirror. Plus, deep down, you feel the same way. Listen to your intuition and go into self-reflection mode. You'll end up finding out so much about yourself in the end.

William: I had some of the same needy tendencies. The thing you can get addicted to is the *perceived* feeling of security that comes with intimacy. Being in a relationship usually means having a close friend and confidant. You are looking for a person who cares and fulfills your needs. However, immediately going from one relationship to another, and being afraid of being alone, is a problem. There is a serious lack of security going on here. Yep. You need to slow your roll and be cool with doing you. Date for the right reasons, and don't kid yourself.

11.
Epilogue: The Finals

Just because you're six feet tall doesn't mean you're done growing.

The Three R's: William

It's all about the three R's: ***reflect, rebound, and rise up***.

I've been around the block—many failed relationships, plus a few marriages under my belt. Did I want to throw in the towel and give up on finding love?

No.

This answer may surprise you, but it's true. I may have felt sad, disappointed, and even angry, but my main focus was always on ***reflection***. What went wrong? Did I learn anything? Am I ready for a relationship or should I focus on "me" time? What do I need that I didn't get? What kind of woman is best suited for me? These questions helped during the healing process and also improved my dating game. In the end, I always felt more confident that I would find my dream lady.

Once the reflection process happened and I felt my "swagga" come back, I knew it was time to ***rebound***. I starting hanging out again, getting phone numbers, and going out on dates. In other words, I ***rose up*** and didn't let the past get in the way of a brighter future.

Forget your age or how many heartaches you have to your name. Love is love and it finds everyone as long as you're willing to search.

Discover Your Happiness: Lauren

As I write these words my heart is heavy because I recently decided to stop dating someone I love. I wasn't fully satisfied with my life, and this unhappiness came out throughout our dating relationship.

From that experience, it's clear that until I find peace within myself, I can't realistically expect to achieve a fulfilling relationship.

And my therapist agrees.

Find your own happiness and live in it. Then, once you feel right at home, start allowing peeps to come in and chill for a while.

The Last Golden Nugget

Lauren and William: *Remain positive—and stay in the flow.* You've probably heard this phrase used in the realm of sports, but we're using it for finding your ultimate match. Staying in the flow is what dating is all about, and we each have to make an effort to create a strategy that's best for us. Then take it and go all the way. Remember that trophy we talked about in the first chapter, and how getting it depends on surviving the Playoffs and entering the Finals? When you get there, you've won. Well, you have the trophy and now it's about raising the stakes. Do you want to seal the deal or what?

Winners like you keep going and keep improving to get even better. Now live what you've learned so that you can take home that championship *ring.*

We're all at different stages of the game, and that's okay. Some of you may be seeing a man or woman you really like, but have frozen up because you're afraid to express how much you care. Others may have their Top 5 List written down and displayed prominently on their nightstand, but still haven't found the courage to go out and use it.

In both scenarios you'd be into the championships and should be proud. You've done great work and reflection. To get the ring, it's all about working on getting to the next level. How? Always do the thing that scares your heart the most. Yep, that's what it takes.

You picked up this book because you have a strong desire to find love. So do all that you can to achieve it, but don't force it. Good things come to those who wait. But don't wait too long. Life is short, and you don't want to spend it in your Cave.

The past is the past, and this moment is a new moment. You have the power to create a long-lasting and truly fulfilling relationship. Use it.

.